100
THINGS TO DO IN
WASHINGTON STATE
BEFORE YOU
DIE

View from Chuckanut Drive

100 THINGS TO DO IN WASHINGTON STATE BEFORE YOU DIE

GINA TARNACKI

REEDY PRESS

Reedy Press
PO Box 5131
St. Louis, MO 63139, USA
reedypress.com

Library of Congress Control Number: 2024949027

ISBN: 9781681065731

Design by Jill Halpin

Cover photo courtesy of Gina Tarnacki.

Unless otherwise noted, all photos are courtesy of the author or are believed to be in the public domain.

Printed in the United States of America
25 26 27 28 29 5 4 3 2 1

DEDICATION

For my grandmas:

My kind, wise Granny, who instilled a
love of books and curiosity in me.

My strong, gentle Grandma Margaret, who left me with an
ongoing desire to know more about my heritage.

Oysterville Sea Farms Patio

CONTENTS

Music and Entertainment

Sports and Recreation

Culture and History

ACKNOWLEDGMENTS

One thing that I was already aware of but that became even clearer to me as I worked on this book is how important the Indigenous tribes of Washington are to the state. I want to take a moment to acknowledge that Washington is on the ancestral land of many Native American tribes, of which there are 29 federally recognized tribal governments. These tribes are Chehalis, Colville, Cowlitz, Kalispel, Hoh, Lummi, Lower Elwha Klallam, Jamestown S'Klallam, Makah, Muckleshoot, Nisqually, Nooksack, Puyallup, Port Gamble S'Klallam, Quileute, Quinault, Samish, Sauk-Suiattle, Shoalwater Bay, Skokomish, Snoqualmie, Spokane, Squaxin Island, Stillaguamish, Suquamish, Swinomish, Tulalip, Upper Skagit, and Yakama. You can learn more about each tribe at washingtontribes.org. The land of Washington is sacred for these tribes, and many of their tribal members are passionate about restoring and protecting the waters, land, and animals in Washington, which is something we should all do.

With that in mind, as you check these items off your list, please remember to recreate responsibly. Most Washingtonians are passionate about nature—it's one of the reasons I love living here among like-minded people who love the outdoors! But with exploration comes responsibility. Follow Leave No Trace rules and you should be golden as you navigate the wilderness areas of the state (lnt.org/why/7-principles).

I also appreciate all the local business owners and employees who give such wonderful character to so many of Washington's cities and towns while providing excellent experiences and activities.

Thanks to Reedy Press for this opportunity to become even more well-acquainted with my cherished home state and providing a platform to help others to do so as well. Special thanks to Barbara and Jaime for helping turn the manuscript into a well-edited and attractive book, and to Amanda for all your ideas and support with the book planning and promotion process.

Also, big shout-out to Alex, Brianna, Jenny, and my cherished book club for listening to me talk their ears off about what should go into this book and providing invaluable advice and tips! Erika and Caitlin, thank you for your expert hiking feedback! Plus, a huge thank-you to my parents, siblings, and Joelene for your never-ending support. (And Mom, you'll always be my favorite beta reader!)

And last but certainly not least, thank you to my husband and daughters for not minding me being gone nearly every weekend over the course of four months to travel around Washington and make sure I had everything covered. Well, maybe they minded a little, ha! Tom, Audrey, Livi: You three bring me so much joy, and I'm so lucky to get to experience Washington and the rest of the world alongside you.

PREFACE

When I began researching and writing this book, I had so many friends, family, and neighbors helpfully answer my questions and tell me their favorite things about Washington or provide more insight on a destination. It was usually followed up with interest about how long this sort of book takes to write. I always responded that writing was the easy part! Researching and trying to narrow down all the incredible things to do in Washington to a list of only 100 was the hard part.

I modified my list of 100 Things to Do in Washington for months until, finally, my patient husband told me just to finalize it and be done because I wouldn't please everyone, anyway. That is probably true, but . . .

Dear reader, I definitely tried! One thing that guided me in narrowing down the list was trying to choose the things that help make Washington the distinct state it is. What are things that can only be found or experienced in Washington? What activities and sites help you better understand the culture and history of Washington? Those were the questions going through my mind as I researched this book.

Discovering locally owned and community-focused places was also important to me as I traveled all over the state. I wanted to make sure I included a wide range of places and hidden gems even in the smallest pockets of Washington. I came across so many wonderful places during my travels and conversations with longtime locals. Sadly, not all of them made it into this book, which easily could have turned into 1,000 Things to Do. I had to make some hard cuts, but I squeezed in as many "extras" as I could! I think the final list of 100 will give readers of this book a journey through Washington that uncovers every side of this multifaceted state, whether you're new to Washington or have lived here your whole life.

I've lived here for a decade now, and while researching this book I was constantly reminded how lucky I am to live in the Pacific Northwest (PNW) and how much I love Washington.

I hope you have fun going through this and checking off all the things to do! I sure had fun writing it. Thanks for reading, and cheers to happy adventures in Washington!

Leavenworth

Bale Breaker Brewing Company

FOOD AND DRINK

1

INDULGE YOUR SWEET TOOTH AT BOEHM'S

History unfolds in a chocolatey fashion at Boehm's Candies in Issaquah. Located down an unassuming side street a short distance from downtown Issaquah, Boehm's is a chocolate wonderland that has roots dating back to 1942 . . . and farther all the way to Austria and Switzerland, where its founder, Julius Boehm, immigrated from in 1941. The candy shop is in Boehm's Edelweiss Chalet, where you'll feel transported to Europe when you pull up and see this traditional alpine chalet that was the first of its kind in Washington. Step through the doors and you'll find the Swiss ambiance extends to the interior decor and uniforms of the friendly staff. On a summer day, order a chocolate-dipped ice cream bar and enjoy it while you walk around the grounds, which include the chocolate factory and a historic cathedral modeled after a 12th-century chapel in St. Moritz, Switzerland, plus informational plaques about the history of the property and Boehm's. Oh, and the chocolate? Decadent deliciousness! Try perennial favorites behind the counter or a box of the whiskey- or balsamic-infused chocolate truffles. Classes and guided tours of the factory and property are also offered.

255 NE Gilman Blvd., Issaquah, 425-392-6652
boehmscandies.com

2

START AND END YOUR DAY
AT THE MUSE WHISKEY & COFFEE

Dreamy Victorian design intermingles with whiskey and fancy coffee at the Muse Whiskey & Coffee, located on the Everett Waterfront. The Muse is a newer establishment, yet the building is dripping with nostalgic history, and it has quickly proven itself worthy of inclusion as one of the top things to do in Washington. A big part of this is due to the painstaking attention to detail that went into refurbishing the more than 100-year-old Weyerhaeuser building. It's now a gorgeous blend of rooms decorated in teal-hued leather, fireplaces, and period art pieces. The water views out the window don't hurt either, especially when enjoying them from the outdoor patio. Breakfast is a relaxed affair (try a cortado paired with a brioche cinnamon roll), while dinner is a much more refined experience that requires a reservation. For dinner, the Muse barroom transforms into a 21-plus speakeasy-style establishment. Try some creative cocktails alongside hearty and thoughtfully curated small bites.

615 Millwright Lp. N, Everett
thewhiskeymuse.com

3

ORDER A PIZZA WITH FRESHLY MADE INGREDIENTS AT THE CARLSON BLOCK

Eat pizza made the way it should be—fresh and from scratch—at the Carlson Block. Located along the main corridor of the small town of Wilkeson, the Carlson Block is located in an historic hotel and specializes in some of the freshest pizza around. The main thing that sets their gourmet pizza pies apart from the rest are the ingredients crafted in-house. Sourdough crust is made daily and used only for pizza ordered that day. Once the dough is gone, the pizza is out for the day. Luckily, that only happens if it's a super busy day, but it's smart to get there early. On nonbusy days, you can also call ahead for your pizza. The Carlson Block is a family-owned business that has pride in all their ingredients, even beyond the crust. Sausage is cured in-house, while mozzarella and produce are sourced from local dairies and farmers.

531 Church St., Wilkeson, 360-761-7593
carlsonblock.com

4

FIND YOUR FAVORITE

HARD CIDER OR APPLE JUICE MADE IN WASHINGTON

Sweet, tangy, mellow, sparkling . . . the components of a superb Washington apple are varied, depending what you're in the mood for. While it's hard to beat biting into a lush, perfectly ripe apple, it can also be just as effervescent to sip an expertly crafted cider drink—whether it's hard cider or alcohol-free juice. There are numerous cideries and orchards around the state, and tasting your way through them to find your personal favorite is a fun pastime. Some standout apple brewsters include the sprawling Finnriver Farm & Cidery, with multiple buildings, beer gardens, and views over the orchards; family-owned Ilwaco Cider Company on the Long Beach Peninsula, which has a big focus on dry ciders crafted by its innovative female cider master; and Bellewood Farms in Lynwood, where you can pick your own apples or get a steaming cup of cider in the on-site café (or a "farm-to-glass" Honeycrisp apple vodka in the distillery).

Finnriver Farm & Cidery
124 Center Rd., Chimacum
360-339-8478
finnriver.com

Ilwaco Cider Company
116 Spruce St. E, Ilwaco
360-777-1933
ilwacociderco.com

Bellewood Farms
6140 Guide Meridian Rd., Lynden
360-318-7720
bellewoodfarms.com

5

ORDER COUGAR GOLD

WITH A SIDE SCOOP OF ICE CREAM AT FERDINAND'S

When a neighbor who went to Washington State University in Pullman told me I had to try Cougar Gold and seemed surprised I'd never heard of it, I quickly looked into this mystery cheese. Well, turns out there's nothing mysterious about it, and it has quite the cult following of both alumni and visitors alike. Cougar Gold is the signature cheese made in-house by students at the university (and then marketed and managed by students as well). It is an unprocessed sharp cheddar that is aged at least one year. The freshest way to get it? With a visit to Ferdinand's Ice Cream Shoppe, the school's very own cheese and ice cream café. What makes Ferdinand's so neat is that you can order some ice cream, get a bag of curds or a round tin of cheese to take home, and then walk up a short flight of stairs to a viewing window, where you can see students working in the WSU Creamery below. The cheese they're making is what will eventually be sold at Ferdinand's and markets around the state. Let's not forget the ice cream, though! Ferdinand's ice cream is made in-house and has a thick, creamy texture with rotating flavors.

2035 NE Ferdinand's Ln., Pullman, 509-335-2141
creamery.wsu.edu/ferdinands-ice-cream-shoppe

MORE SWEET DAIRY TREATS IN WASHINGTON

(Most of these places have dairy-free options, too!)

Amethyst Creamery, Richland

Delicious ice cream served up alongside a collection of rocks and gems.

facebook.com/AmethystCreamery

Granny's Cafe, Port Angeles

Famously good soft serve in chocolate, vanilla, or a swirl.

grannyscafe.net

Humble Cow Ice Cream, Olympia

Small-batch ice cream maker in a cheerful setting with scoops and ice cream cookie sandwiches.

humblecowicecream.com

Island Cool

Ice cream with lots of topping options in Kingston, Bainbridge Island, and Poulsbo, plus a froyo shop in Bainbridge.

island-cool.com

Lopez Island Creamery, Anacortes

Artisanal ice cream available in scoops, pints, and sandwiches.

lopezislandcreamery.com

Mallard Ice Cream, Bellingham

Fresh, eclectic flavors in downtown Bellingham.

mallardicecream.com

Molly Moon's

Popular local chain in Seattle and surrounding suburbs.

mollymoon.com

Pete & Belle's, Spokane Valley

Two locations serving up creamy ice cream with real ingredients.

petebelles.com

6

BITE INTO FRUITY CHOCOLATES
AT CHUKAR CHERRIES

Instead of farm to table, it's farm to chocolate-cherries-melting-in-your-mouth at Chukar Cherries. A visit to Chukar Cherries' flagship store and headquarters in Prosser is not your typical chocolate-tasting experience. Step into the shop and you'll see cherry-infused items lining the shelves alongside friendly employees. A lot of the products are chocolate related, but you'll also find salsa, pie fillings, grilling marinades, granola, candied nuts, and more. As you shop, a tasting concierge appears with bowls of different chocolates and uses tongs to place chocolate onto your palm with a description of the flavors you'll notice while chewing. It feels a lot like wine tasting, but with chocolates. While tasting, you'll learn more about the owners, who were inspired by watching old cherries shrivel on their trees and wanting to figure out how to use that fruit so they didn't go to waste. The result . . . Chukar Cherries!

320 Wine Country Rd., Prosser, 509-786-2055
chukar.com

TIP

Fruit growing isn't just for the inland areas of Washington. The Long Beach Peninsula has ideal conditions for growing cranberries. During fall, you can even see farmers wading into the cranberry bogs to harvest the seeds. For a sweet treat any time of year, visit the museum and gift shop at the Pacific Coast Cranberry Research Foundation for some homemade cranberry ice cream.

2907 Pioneer Rd., Long Beach, 360-642-5553
cranberrymuseum.com

7

TREAT YOURSELF
TO A SLICE OF WHIDBEY PIE

Whidbey Pies has a special place in my family's heart. For my husband's birthday, instead of cake, I put candles in a cherry Whidbey pie because it's one of his favorite desserts. I typically purchase the pie from our local market, but the best way to enjoy a slice is with a visit to Whidbey Pies' flagship bakery on its namesake island. Located in the harbor town of Langley on the east side of Whidbey Island, you'll walk into Whidbey Pies' cozy shop and immediately be greeted by sumptuous smells permeating around the farmhouse-style café. Whidbey Pies is family owned, and that familial feel translates into service, as the friendly staff dish up an assortment of pies ranging from apple to marionberry to Whidbey-grown loganberry. They also use plant-based compostable containers instead of plastic for pies to go.

111 Anthes Ave., Langley, 360-221-6875
whidbeypies.com

TIP

Whidbey Pies used to operate out of the café at the landmark Greenbank Farm on the other side of Whidbey Island in Freeland. They no longer reside there, but their pies are still sold by the new owners, who now operate Old Spots Bistro, a great place for lunch (and pie for dessert) in a garden setting next to an old converted red barn.

765 Wonn Rd., Greenbank, 360-222-3797

8

BEER TASTE
BY HOP FIELDS AT
BALE BREAKER BREWING COMPANY

Sip some local craft beer while looking at the fields that produced the hops at Bale Breaker Brewing Company in Yakima. This farm-to-bar brewing company puts a focus on local hops with an assortment of beers on tap, including ones made from freshly harvested hops. Walking from the parking lot to the entrance past hop fields is a neat way to start a beer-tasting adventure. Inside, the large wood tables that open seamlessly onto the beer garden make for a relaxing and fun place. Local food trucks are often parked outside for an easy dinner to pair with your pint. The service is friendly and informative, which helps if you're not sure what brews to try. I happened to be there the evening before their annual Post Harvest Festival, which celebrates the hardworking hop farmers. Sadly, I couldn't stay long, but it looked like a rocking good time with music and local food vendors. At the event, it was clear that the brewing and farm community in Yakima plus all their customers are very important to Bale Breaker.

1801 Birchfield Rd., Yakima, 509-424-4000
balebreaker.com

DID YOU KNOW?

Washington's Yakima Valley grows 75 percent of the country's hops and is known as the Hops Capital of the World.

MORE BREWERIES WITH BEER GARDENS TO CHECK OUT

Cowiche Creek Brewing Company

514 Thompson Rd., Cowiche, 509-678-0324
cowichecreekbrewing.com

South Fork

14303 436th Ave. SE, North Bend, 425-292-3614
southforknorthbend.com

Snoqualmie Falls Brewery

8032 Falls Ave. SE, Snoqualmie, 425-831-2357
fallsbrew.com

Palouse Brewing Company

335 E Main St., Palouse, 509-878-1444
facebook.com/people/Palouse-Brewing-Company/100087207236278

Blackbeard's Brewing

700 W Ocean Ave., Westport, 360-268-7662
blackbeardsbrewing.com

Icicle Brewing Company

935 Front St., Leavenworth, 509-548-2739
iciclebrewing.com

Big Block Brewing

3310 E Lake Sammamish Pkwy., Sammamish
425-270-3757
bigblockbrewery.com

Wander Brewing

1807 Dean Ave., Bellingham, 360-647-6152
wanderbrewing.com

9

TRY THE GEODUCK,
A PACIFIC NORTHWEST DELICACY

Taylor Shellfish Farms is a western Washington institution that has been owned and operated by the Taylor family for five generations. The company is known for their steadfast attention to providing fresh local seafood via their (own) farm-to-table collection of markets and oyster bars. The one uniquely Northwest delicacy you need to try there is the geoduck (pronounced gooey-duck). It can grow up to nine inches long and weigh up to ten pounds. Geoducks can be found along the whole Pacific Coast but are predominantly found in the waters off Washington and British Columbia. Taylor Shellfish fosters the spawning, growth, and harvesting of these clams (which take about six years to reach maturity in the sand) by hand. Then they serve up these large clams at one of their Seattle oyster bars (Pioneer Square, Capitol Hill, or Queen Anne) or markets (Samish or Shelton). Geoduck probably looks like no clam you've had before—which is part of the fun! So put your tastebuds' qualms aside and try one of Washington's most elusive foods.

360-426-6178
taylorshellfishfarms.com

TIP

Taylor Shellfish is also a good place to get fresh Dungeness crab.

10

SIP SOME SPIRITS
AT CHUCKANUT BAY DISTILLERY

Right in the heart of downtown Bellingham is a distillery making waves and winning awards in the world of alcohol spirits. That distillery is Chuckanut Bay Distillery, and their warm and welcoming tasting room and restaurant are both great places to try their liquors. The Muzzleflash Whiskey is expertly blended with locally grown corn, rye, and wheat that's triple distilled and aged in Chuckanut Bay barrels for a traditional whiskey with an American twist. The distillery's bourbon, gin, and vodka have also won various spirits awards. That said, it's the amber liquid in the bottle with the mythical creature on it you'll have to try: the Krampus Herbal Liqueur. It is a perfect blend of winter spice with a tangy honey aftertaste. Krampus is a great holiday spirit mixed with hot cider or a cold apple or pear wine. (Yes, I know this from my own holiday party experience!)

1311 Cornwall Ave., Bellingham, 360-738-7179
chuckanutbaydistillery.com

TIP

Chuckanut Bay Distillery's tasting room is connected to its restaurant, Penny Farthing. This is a great place to eat even if you're not a liquor person, with locally sourced ingredients and one of the best queso dips around.

11

ORDER A GIANT, GOOEY CINNAMON ROLL

AT THE MALTBY CAFE

Breakfast is served all day at the Maltby Cafe in Snohomish. That means ample opportunities for ordering some of the best waffles, egg dishes, and other homestyle-menu options around. Though you may want to bypass all that and go straight for the sweet stuff, which in the Maltby Cafe's case means its famous cinnamon rolls. You get your money's worth and then some with these cinnamon rolls, which are hand rolled each day. The cinnamon rolls are large enough that just one can easily satisfy a family of four . . . and probably have leftovers. The Maltby Cafe has been around for over 35 years and is located in what used to be a gymnasium for the former school building next door. In 1988, the Maltby Cafe was purchased by three local women who still own and operate it today.

8809 Maltby Rd., Snohomish, 425-483-3123
maltbycafe.com

GET A BURGER TO GO
AT DICK'S

Dick's Drive-In is the Washington answer to that other West Coast burger chain staple, In-N-Out. But instead of having a secret menu of modifications, Dick's is all about NO modifications. Which is kind of part of the fun. The reason for that is so they can keep the ordering process quick and affordable. Dick's has substantially grown from when its original location in Seattle's Wallingford District opened in 1954, but it is still only located in Washington, mostly along the I-5 corridor. Why? The original owners (one of whom is the namesake for the company) said they were family men who didn't want to travel and did want to focus their growth on their hometown of Seattle. That community and family mindset combined with a menu that has barely changed in 70 years has kept Dick's Drive-In's customers coming back again and again—and continuing to make new loyal customers.

206-634-0300
ddir.com

13

FEAST YOUR WAY
THROUGH PYBUS PUBLIC MARKET

This covered market and food hall is the perfect destination for trying new local businesses year-round. Bring your friends or family, grab a table in the communal area, and then feast on local wine, beer, and treats both savory and sweet. Pybus Public Market covers 26,000 square feet in a refurbished steel warehouse next to the Columbia River. The space hosts more than 15 permanent vendors, with additional rotating food trucks often parked outside. On Saturdays, the permanent offerings extend into a farmers market with fresh local produce available for sale. A rotating artist spotlight also keeps new craftsmen creations coming into Pybus for consumers to discover. The vendors at Pybus Public Market provide a lot of comfort food favorites, from Neapolitan pizza and gourmet burgers to authentic avocado toast and carnitas. For dessert, there are vendors selling ice cream and pastries. To drink, check out one of the beer or wine tasting rooms.

3 N Worthen St., Wenatchee, 509-888-3900
pybuspublicmarket.org

EAT IN A MILK BOTTLE
IN SPOKANE

Delight in some dairy-ific architecture when you dine in a milk bottle in Spokane. Yes, a milk bottle. Mary Lou's Milk Bottle restaurant resides inside a building designed to look like a massive container of that creamy white liquid. The beloved Spokane institution is reminiscent of a retro diner, with classic American cuisine like burgers and chili on the menu. Plus, it wouldn't be an appropriate milk bottle–shaped restaurant without some iconic dairy treats. Delicious milkshakes and other ice cream desserts perfectly round out the dining experience at Mary Lou's Milk Bottle. Wondering what spurred the interesting building design? It goes back to 1935, when it was built to sell local dairy products. It wasn't until 1991 that it became an ice cream parlor and eventual diner. Today, the milk bottle charm remains outside and in, such as the lights made from recycled milk bottles hanging from the ceiling.

802 W Garland Ave., Spokane, 509-325-1772
marylous.org

15

SUPPORT INDEPENDENT COFFEE SHOPS

As the birthplace of Starbucks and 1990s coffee culture, Washington is no stranger to a frothy latte. And while I do have the Starbucks app on my phone for those busy grab-and-go days, when possible, I prefer getting my half-vanilla, whole-milk latte from an independent coffee shop. It puts money back into the local community, and the great ones also give you a clear sense of the neighborhood vibe and culture. My go-to local coffee shop when I want to meet up with friends or get in a good work session is Aroma Coffee Co. in Fall City, which is located in an old house that has been remodeled with modern farmhouse style and has plenty of indoor and outdoor seating. And if I lived in the Tri-Cities, the book lover in me would probably hang out constantly at Novel Coffee and Teas in Richland, which is decorated in soothing colors and books, and makes the perfect creamy latte with signature espresso drink names like Typewriter and Author.

Aroma Coffee Co.
33429 SE Redmond–Fall City Rd., Fall City, 425-441-8111
aromacoffeeco.com

Novel Coffee and Teas
950 George Washington Way, Richland, 509-420-4094

MORE LOCAL COFFEE SHOPS TO GET YOUR CAFFEINE FIX FROM

Apothecary Coffee

339 Ferry St., Sedro-Woolley, 360-853-2003
apothecarycoffeerx.com

Blue Star Coffee Roasters

1240 E Methow Valley Hwy., Twisp, 509-997-2583
bluestarcoffeeroasters.com

Temple Pastries

2524 S Jackson St., Seattle
templepastries.com

Cot's Peak Coffee

22 E Second St., Naches
509-955-3676
cotspeakcoffee.com

Looking Glass Coffee

801 First St., Unit 201, Snohomish, 360-863-3557
lookingglasscoffee.com

Ristretto Coffee Lounge & Wine Bar

416 S First St., Mount Vernon, 360-336-0951
ristrettocoffeemv.com

Roost Coffee

125 SE Spring St., #102, Pullman, 509-332-8534
roostcoffeepullman.com

Samayra Coffee Co.

1600 Cooper Point Rd. SW, Ste. 630, Olympia
360-338-0926
samayracoffee.com

Topside Coffee Cabin

215 Wilkes St., Ste. 102, Steilacoom, 253-301-3323
topsidebargrill.com/topside-coffee-cabin-old-1

Wake 'n' Bakery

6903 Bourne St., Deming,
360-599-1658
wakenbakeryglacier.com

Walla Walla Roastery

290 A St., Walla Walla
509-526-3211
wwroastery.com

16

EAT THE FRESHEST OYSTERS
IN OYSTERVILLE

I'm the type of oyster connoisseur who thought if I just kept trying them I would eventually develop a taste for these slimy sea creatures. That wasn't really happening . . . until I visited Willapa Bay. I went to Oysterville Sea Farms and suddenly understood the hype for oysters. The oysters there are quite mild, with minimal brine and just a hint of sweetness. The shellfish are delicious on their own but served alongside lemon and cocktail sauce they're amazingly tasty. This might be because they're as fresh as you can get. Willapa Bay happens to be one of the cleanest bays in the world, and Oysterville Sea Farms puts a big focus on continuing to keep the bay clean and farming the oysters in a sustainable manner. The oysters are literally farmed from the waters of the bay lapping against the back patio of the restaurant. Making the dining experience even better is getting to look at that gorgeous view while sitting inside by the laid-back oyster bar or the large back patio with a beer or a cup of delicious homemade clam chowder to enjoy alongside your oysters.

34300 First St., Oysterville, 360-665-6585
willapawild.com

TIP

Another excellent place to get fresh, local oysters in Washington is Hama Hama Oyster Saloon on Hood Canal.

35846 US-101, Ste. B, Lilliwaup, 360-877-5811
hamahamaoysters.com

17

STASH THE KEYS
AND WALK BETWEEN WINERIES

Part of the fun of wine tasting is going to multiple wineries in a day to compare varietals. But if you don't want to do rock paper scissors for a designated driver or pay for an expensive charter service to drive you around, fear not—Washington's wine regions have you covered. There are several wine neighborhoods in Washington that have multiple tasting rooms within walking distance of each other, plus lodging nearby or an affordable rideshare fare away. Some are right in downtown areas while others are nestled in scenic areas on the outskirts of town, providing a tasting experience for every style traveler. Must-visit tasting room blocks include Woodinville (downtown or the Schoolhouse area), Prosser (Vintners Village and Prosser Wine & Food Park), Kennewick (Columbia Gardens Wine and Artisan Village), Richland (Tulip Lane), Walla Walla (downtown and by the airport), and Yakima (Old North Yakima Historic District).

stateofwatourism.com/wine-country

FILL YOUR PANTRY
WITH GOODIES FROM COUNTRY MERCANTILE

Inside Country Mercantile, the charm of a general store of olden days mixed with modern aspects like a sandwich counter and friendly service await. Country Mercantile's specialty is its rows and rows of canned vegetables, jams, and spreads—although kids will probably make a beeline for the jars of bulk candy. Complementing the gummies, licorice, and other sugary candies are large display cases with a variety of chocolate confections made in-house. The family-owned Country Mercantile is based in the Tri-Cities and pays homage to the farmland surrounding the region with fresh fruits and veggies for sale. Farmhouse homewares and decor are also sold in a little side room. If you're in need of an actual meal, sidle up to the counter and order a gourmet sandwich to enjoy at one of the tables in the cozy dining nook.

5015 Ava Way, Richland, 509-581-0306
232 Crestloch Rd., Pasco, 509-545-2192
countrymercantile.com

19

FEAST ON FINE DINING WITH A PNW TWIST
AT HERBFARM

When you're dropping several hundred dollars on dinner at an eight-course, fine-dining restaurant with white tablecloths and wine pairings, you probably expect you should pull out your finest cocktail attire and uncomfortable shoes. Not so at Herbfarm, a restaurant that puts your comfort first and where slacks and a well-tailored plaid shirt are just as fine as a suit or fancy dress. Herbfarm just wants you to be comfortable. But enough about the dress code. Let's talk about the food—that's where the magic of Herbfarm truly blooms. The restaurant has its own on-site garden that it utilizes along with other locally sourced ingredients for its impressive set menu. The meal begins with an informal talk from the chef about that night's meal, and it truly feels like you're just having a big dinner at the home of some fancy acquaintance with an impressive wine cellar. If Herbfarm doesn't sound like your cup of tea, check out the also highly rated Barking Frog next door. It utilizes the same garden with expert culinary skills, but the menu and ambiance are more approachable and affordable.

14590 NE 145th St., Woodinville, 425-485-5300
theherbfarm.com

TIP

Want to get all dressed up? Then make reservations (well ahead of time, especially around the holidays) to dine at Canlis, a long-standing, family-owned fine-dining establishment in Seattle that has gourmet dishes, five-star service, stunning views of Lake Union, and a fancy dress code.

2576 Aurora Ave. N, Seattle, 206-283-3313
canlis.com

20

SIP SOME RED BUBBLY
WHILE ENJOYING VINEYARD VIEWS AT TREVERI CELLARS

Treveri Cellars is an up-and-coming maker of sparkling wines. Before you write off another too-sweet bubbly, check this place out. Treveri Cellars makes only sparkling wines, and their attention to detail with these wines is exquisite. Their sparkling wines range from a common brut to a sparkling Syrah that's a surprising deep-red shade. For those who prefer the tastes of red wine but bemoan it on a hot summer day, this 100 percent Syrah sparkling wine is a must-try. The winery tasting room also has small eats. The baguette with sweet-herbed honey butter pairs delightfully with the sweeter wines on the menu. Drinking or not, you'll enjoy soaking up the incredible views of Yakima Valley's rolling hills from the tasting room's large terrace.

71 Gangl Rd., Wapato, 509-877-0925
trevericellars.com

TIP

Tirriddis Sparkling Wines in Prosser is another burgeoning sparkling wine hot spot in Washington.

2140-B Wine Country Rd., Prosser, 509-502-8576
tirriddis.com

EXPAND YOUR PALATE
WITH INTERNATIONAL FARE ACROSS THE STATE

Washington is an incredible blend of cultures and backgrounds. This bubbles over into the cuisine of the state, with an amazing array of tastes inspired by all corners of the globe. My favorite international restaurants do a wonderful job at weaving culture with high-quality cuisine. At the top of this list is Andreas Keller Restaurant in Leavenworth, which heavily plays into the Bavarian theme of the town without seeming kitschy. The authentic German cuisine is well crafted while the interior feels cozy and festive while you're serenaded by lively accordion players. Another favorite is Los Hernández Tamales in Union Gap, a welcoming little restaurant that serves up homemade (and James Beard winning!) tamales available for takeout or dining in. And while we're on the subject of delicious Mexican cuisine, don't miss Pita's Taqueria in Enumclaw. This window-order eatery is a bit awkwardly fit into the back parking lot of a gas station, but don't let that deter you. Pita's serves up incredibly filling and tasty authentic Mexican street food.

Andreas Keller Restaurant
829 Front St., Leavenworth
509-548-6000
andreaskellerrestaurant.com

Los Hernández Tamales
3706 Main St., Union Gap
509-457-6003
loshernandeztamales.com

Pita's Taqueria
1547 McHugh Ave., Enumclaw, 360-226-3273
pitastaqueriawa.com

MORE INTERNATIONAL FARE TO TRY

Europa Italian & Spanish Cuisine

Delicious pasta and paella dishes with vegetarian options.

2459 S Union Pl., Ste. 110, Kennewick, 509-579-5828
europaitalianspanish.com

Seatango Argentine Bakery & Cafe

Mom-and-pop-style bakery serving up empanadas and other Argentine treats.

12728 Lake City Way NE, Seattle, 206-327-9787
seatangofoods.com

The Pink Door

Upscale Italian cuisine in a unique setting with nightly cabaret shows.

1919 Post Alley, Seattle
206-443-3241
thepinkdoor.net

SuperKim Crab House

Family-owned restaurant blending the art of Thai street food with Cajun flair. Award-winning clam chowder plus fresh seafood entrées.

460 106th Ave. NE, Bellevue, 425-969-3635 & 166 S King St., Seattle 206-656-5936
superkimcrabhouse.com

Sushi Kashiba

Crafting Edomae sushi under the direction of Seattle's first sushi master. Dining room plus in-demand chef's counter seating.

86 Pine St., Ste. #1, Seattle
206-441-8844
sushikashiba.com

Kanishka Cuisine of India

Authentic Indian cuisine in two locations.

16651 Redmond Way, Ste. 180, Redmond, 425-869-9182
22406 Pacific Hwy., S, Des Moines, 425-477-7771
kanishkaredmond.com

Salmon Run at Issaquah Salmon Hatchery

MUSIC AND ENTERTAINMENT

22

REMINISCE ABOUT '90S ROM-COMS IN THE STADIUM DISTRICT

If your teenage dreams were also filled with visions of Heath Ledger strutting down stadium steps while serenading the hard-to-get girl, then your '90s-loving heart is going to enjoy a visit to the Stadium District in Tacoma. The main claim to fame is Stadium High School, a public school so fabulous I assumed it was a movie set while watching *10 Things I Hate About You* over 25 years ago. But, nope, that prime bit of real estate overlooking the harbor is attended by teenagers every school day. Consider visiting during off-school hours for a walk around the exterior of the château-style building (originally built in 1891 to be a hotel) and a glimpse through the Gothic gates of that iconic sports field Ledger and the movie made famous. Once you're done with your movie nostalgia, walk a few minutes to Art House Cafe for one of the best brunches in Washington. Complete the trifecta of your Stadium District visit with a stop at the family-owned Ranko's Pharmacy, a gift shop and pharmacy in one with a nod to retro nostalgia.

Stadium High School
111 N E St., Tacoma
253-571-3100
stadium.tacomaschools.org

Art House Cafe
111 N Tacoma Ave., Tacoma
253-212-2011
arthousecafe.com

Ranko's Pharmacy
101 N Tacoma Ave., Tacoma
253-383-2411
facebook.com/rankospharmacy

TIP

For more film culture in Washington, head to Forks for *Twilight* memorabilia and Snoqualmie/North Bend for *Twin Peaks* film locales.

SPOT ORCAS
IN THE WILD

Who needs a screen in Washington when we have our own National Geographic documentary just waiting for us on Puget Sound? Seattle is home to both transient and Southern Resident orcas. You can seek a glimpse of orcas two ways: on a whale-watching tour or on your own. The latter is my favorite way, but if short on time, the whale-watching boat is often successful. Choose a reputable tour operator, like Maya's Legacy Whale Watching, which follows the proper whale regulations and protocols for boaters. When it comes to spotting orcas on your own, social media can be a big help. Pages like the Orca Network Community Group are full of orca-loving individuals who teach how to respectfully observe orcas and where these magnificent creatures have recently been spotted. Or book a room somewhere by Lime Kiln Point State Park on San Juan Island or a vacation rental along Hood Canal for a week, grab your binoculars, and cross your fingers that orcas pass by during your stay!

Maya's Legacy Whale Watching
50 Spring St., Ste. 101, Friday Harbor, 360-378-7996
sanjuanislandwhalewatch.com

Lime Kiln Point State Park
1567 West Side Rd., Friday Harbor, 360-378-2044
parks.wa.gov/find-parks/state-parks/lime-kiln-point-state-park

TIP

The beloved Southern Resident orca pods are currently facing a high threat of extinction that is happening before our very eyes. Learn more about the struggles these salmon-eating orcas are facing and steps that can help them at the Whale Museum in Friday Harbor or the Langley Whale Center on Whidbey Island.

whalemuseum.org
orcanetwork.org/langley-whale-center

24

UNCOVER THE MYSTERIES OF SPACE
IN THE TRI-CITIES

The Tri-Cities are known for their STEM-focused facilities, especially where space is involved. Gaze at the stars without going outside at the CPCCo Planetarium in Pasco. This state-of-the-art cinematic experience uses cutting-edge projection technology on the 36-foot panoramic screen to create a 3D experience that doesn't require the usual flimsy glasses. You'll feel immersed in the solar system as a high-definition science film guides you through space and earth on the domed screen. For more space-tastic science, head to the Laser Interferometer Gravitational-Wave Observatory (LIGO) in Richland. LIGO was part of the discovery of the world's first gravitational waves (aka two black holes running into each other over a billion years ago) in 2015. You can visit the LIGO Exploration Center (LExC) to learn more about this incredible occurrence and other space facts through interactive exhibits. Tours of the LIGO Hanford Observatory are also offered monthly.

CPCCo Planetarium
2600 N 20th Ave., Pasco, 509-542-4515
columbiabasin.edu/connect/arts-and-culture/planetarium.html

LIGO
127124 N Rt. 10, Richland, 509-372-8106
ligo.caltech.edu/WA/page/lexc

25

FIND YOUR INNER VIKING
IN "LITTLE NORWAY"

The European-inspired Poulsbo may not be as well known to visitors as its Bavarian counterpart in the Cascades, but it packs in a lot of charm without as many day trippers. Poulsbo's Nordic aesthetic stems from its strong Scandinavian roots. So much so that it has been nicknamed "Little Norway" and even has a couple of official sister cities in Norway. Combine the Norwegian fun with three marinas, a walkable downtown area and waterfront boardwalk, plus delicious eateries and cute boutiques, and you'll soon see why Poulsbo is such an entertaining day trip (or weekend getaway!). It's not all charm and cuteness, though. During the yearly Viking Fest, Poulsbo delightfully transforms into a Viking-themed village with costumes, parades, a street fair, and even a strongman competition. At all times of the year, you can visit the Nordiska shop for Viking and Scandinavian souvenirs, apparel, and home goods.

cityofpoulsbo.com

26

WATCH A LIVE PERFORMANCE

AT THE PARAMOUNT THEATRE

Ornate beauty awaits at the Paramount Theatre in Seattle. This fancy performance hall feels like a step back in time. And in a lot of ways, it is! The theater was built in 1928 as a silent movie house (fun fact: The Paramount has Silent Movie Mondays multiple times a year). The mahogany banister and velvet accents of the lobby are reminiscent of this bygone age. Enter the theater hall and you're greeted with a gilded gold stage standing prominently in front of curving rows of scarlet seats. The acoustics are all modern, though, making the theater an excellent place for music. Broadway shows, dance troupes, and live band performances excel at the Paramount, with the high-quality sound and lighting making each production world class. Because of this, the Paramount Theatre attracts traveling Broadway performances and other top acts from all over the country.

911 Pine St., Seattle, 206-682-1414
stgpresents.org

SUPPORT LOCAL PLAYHOUSES IN WASHINGTON

The Cutter Theatre

302 Park St., Metaline Falls, 509-446-4108
cuttertheatre.com

Lincoln Theatre

712 S First St., Mount Vernon, 360-336-8955
lincolntheatre.org

The Richland Players

608 The Pkwy., Richland, 509-943-1991
richlandplayers.org

River City Playhouse

127 Lake St. SE, Ilwaco
peninsula-players.com

San Juan Community Theatre

100 Second St. N, Friday Harbor, 360-378-3210
sjctheatre.org

Village Theatre

303 Front St. N, Issaquah, and 2710 Wetmore Ave., Everett, 425-392-2202
villagetheatre.org

27

WITNESS THE INCREDIBLE
SALMON RUN

The salmon run is one of the natural world's most incredible feats. Every year, usually between August and October, thousands of salmon leave the ocean and make their way up rivers and creeks to reach the place of their respective births, where they will do their final act of spawning. How the salmon remember this is mind boggling, and so is watching them push against the current to make their way upstream. Washington has many spots where you're likely to see the salmon run. If you're new to the salmon run phenomenon, head to the Issaquah Salmon Hatchery. This is one of the most reputable hatcheries in the Northwest and has incredible docents plus informational panels. The Issaquah Salmon Festival is an especially great time of year to go and learn more from the docents, plus shop at the vendors market. Another great place to see the salmon run without all the fanfare is at Ballard Locks, where you can view fish swimming up the salmon ladder and learn more at the adjacent Salmon Education Center.

125 W Sunset Way, Issaquah, 425-392-1118
issaquahfish.org

3015 NW 54th St., Seattle, 206-780-2500
ballardlocks.org

TIP

The Ballard Locks is also worth visiting any time of year to see boats going through the remarkably engineered system that connects Lake Washington and Lake Union to Puget Sound.

28

WATCH A CONCERT UNDER THE STARS
AT THE GORGE AMPHITHEATRE

The Gorge is an iconic music venue in Washington. Located near the town of George (also worth a visit just for the fun of the town name: get it?), this outdoor amphitheater is located next to the Columbia River and provides one of the most scenic and memorable concert experiences in the state. Whether it's a one-night headliner or a multiday music festival, the Gorge provides an incredible setting of fun and community. The venue can seat 20,000, some on bench-type seats and some in open seating on a terraced lawn overlooking the stage with the river glistening just beyond it.

754 Silica Rd. NW, Quincy, 206-607-3440
gorgeamphitheatre.com

TIP

Pretty much everyone I know who grew up in Washington has fond stories of roughing it in the campgrounds, aka "Tent City," next to the Gorge to save a few bucks. If you're past your partying and no-frills camping days, don't worry—the Gorge is still for you. You can attend a concert and then stay at one of the many hotels in George or vacation rentals around the region. Sagecliffe Resort and Spa is a luxury option in Quincy. There are also upscale glamping options like Gorge Oasis Campground if you like the idea of sleeping under the stars without young 20-somethings partying around the tent next door.

sagecliffferesortandspa.com
gorgeampitheatre.com/camping

29

MUNCH ON POPCORN WITH REAL BUTTER AT THE ROSE THEATRE

The charmingly vintage Rose Theatre has been a part of the Port Townsend community for over 115 years, but the continuation of that legacy recently came into question when the theater was put up for sale by its previous owner, who was ready to retire. Thankfully, a local couple bought the theater to retain its wonderful throwback appeal. The Rose has three different viewing areas with very distinct vibes. The main Rose Theatre is more of your typical movie theater setup, but with a more intimate feel with shorter rows of seats plus a fun balcony overhead. The Rosebud Cinema has Art Deco couch seating and feels like a throwback from the roaring '20s. Upstairs and one door down, the Victorian-inspired Starlight Room has views of Admiralty Inlet and is a popular place to rent for viewing parties or special showings. From the concession stand, don't miss out on getting a bag of popcorn. It's freshly popped, uses real butter, and has a countertop of different spices you can shake on top.

235 Taylor St., Port Townsend, 360-385-1089
rosetheatre.com

TIP

You can stop in just to buy some popcorn even if you aren't seeing a movie.

30

FERRY TO THE EXQUISITE SAN JUAN ISLANDS

Judging by how my kids react each time we step on a ferry (so exciting!), I'm going to put ferry rides down as entertainment in this book. With speed, views, food and drink, and even puzzles—plus the possibility to see orcas or migrating whales—it truly is an entertaining ride. The best ferry, in my opinion, takes you to the incredible San Juan Islands, a place where mountains and ocean truly collide. The San Juans consist of four ferry-accessible islands (plus more than 100 smaller isles) full of nature, adorable towns, and wildlife spotting, both on land and in the water. The namesake island of San Juan is known for its walkable main town, Friday Harbor, and prime orca whale–spotting points. Orcas Island is known for its sprawling, old-growth forest beauty, with many vistas of the sea. Lopez Island and Shaw Island are smaller and quieter, with a focus on the rugged outdoors. The San Juans are a remote, enchanting place where you should definitely spend a weekend at some point in your life (or a month, but who's counting?!).

visitsanjuans.com/washington-state-ferries

31

EMBARK ON A TRAIN RIDE
THROUGH WASHINGTON'S RAILWAY PAST

Washington has a long and varied railroad history dating back to the mid-1800s. For many decades, the rail industry was a big employer for Washington citizens. This became even more prominent in 1873, when the transcontinental railroad officially connected to the West Coast in Tacoma. Though rail travel has drastically changed since the 19th century, there are still some recreational train rides people can do along some of these historic tracks. At the historic building that houses the Snoqualmie Northwest Railway Museum, you can learn more about the history of trains in Washington, walk around antique railcars on the grounds, and board the old-fashioned train for a thrilling ride to North Bend past Snoqualmie Falls, stopping at another railway museum during the journey. On the Mt. Rainier Scenic Railroad, which departs from Elbe, you'll board an open-air vintage steam locomotive that takes you through mountain wilderness with a stop in Mineral. Both of these train lines also offer delightful Christmas-themed trains during the holidays.

Snoqualmie Historic Depot
38625 SE King St., Snoqualmie, 425-888-3030
trainmuseum.org

Mt. Rainier Scenic Railroad
54124 Mountain Hwy. E, Elbe, 253-900-7245
mtrainierrailroad.com

TIP

For some more railroad fun, eat in a converted train depot in Seaview at the Depot Restaurant, or a train car at the Railway Cafe in Blaine.

facebook.com/therailwaycafe
depotrestaurantdining.com

32

LISTEN TO THE SOUNDS OF THE ORCHESTRA
AT THE FOX THEATER

The Fox Theater in Spokane had a creative beginning—it was designed by the same man who drafted the design plan for Old Faithful Inn in Yellowstone National Park. Walk into the Fox and you're immediately wowed by large gold half-sunburst designs that frame the stage, mezzanine balconies, and ceiling. Built in 1931, the Fox served as a performance venue and movie theater for many decades. Today, it is home to the impressively skilled Spokane Symphony, a dynamic orchestra that regularly puts on concerts as the main attraction, or as the background music to ballets, operas, and other performers. The Spokane Symphony plays a wide range of music, from classical pieces to contemporary music reimagined for string instruments. No matter which show you choose, you'll enjoy the powerful sounds of the orchestra while sitting in one of Washington's most opulently gorgeous theaters.

1001 W Sprague Ave., Spokane, 509-624-1200
foxtheaterspokane.org

33

SET UP A PICNIC

AT THE CHATEAU ST. MICHELLE CONCERT SERIES

If you like wine and music—or simply vineyard views and music—it doesn't get any better than a concert at Chateau St. Michelle winery in Woodinville. Chateau St. Michelle is an icon in the Washington wine world, helping to put our state's wines on the map. The winery's summer concert series has been equally iconic. Begun in 1984, it has hosted the likes of the Beach Boys, Sarah McLachlan, Stevie Wonder, John Legend, and so many more musical acts. The vibe of this outdoor concert venue is casual. General admission has open seating along a gently sloping grassy hill facing the stage. You're allowed to bring chairs and blankets. A small area in front of the stage is the reserve ticket section with assigned seats. Food and bottles of Chateau St. Michelle wine are sold on-site, or you can bring your own picnic. Doors open two hours before showtime so you can enjoy the outdoor ambiance before the concert begins. Tickets for the most popular entertainers sell out quickly, so don't delay purchasing if one of your faves is coming this summer!

14111 NE 145th St., Woodinville, 425-488-1133
ste-michelle.com/visit-us/summer-concerts

34

STROLL ALONG
THE VANCOUVER WATERFRONT AND PIER

You can easily spend a whole day on the river waterfront in Vancouver, Washington, and never get bored. With a massive redevelopment in 2018, the scenic waterfront went from charming to fabulous (and still delivers ample charm). It now is home to a bevy of coffee shops, wine tasting rooms, breweries, boutique shops, and seafood restaurants. While popping in and out of these various establishments is part of the fun, the focal point of the Vancouver Waterfront is the Grant Street Pier, an intricately designed cable-stayed pier that has a sailboat reminiscent design. The 90-foot pier provides gorgeous views to the Columbia River. In the summer, plan your visit for Thursday when the Vancouver Waterfront Concert Series hosts live music. Looking for more scenery? Head to the paved Waterfront Renaissance Trail, which goes for five miles and connects the waterfront to downtown Vancouver, taking you past historic shipyards and statues along the way.

Waterfront Way, 503-245-1976
thewaterfrontvancouverusa.com

TIP

The Waterfront connects to Fort Vancouver National Historic Site via the pedestrian Vancouver Land Bridge. The reconstructed fort is also well worth a visit during your time in Vancouver to learn more about the city's past, when the fort served as the regional fur trade headquarters for the Hudson's Bay Company. While visiting the Fort Vancouver National Historic Site, you can also see old army barracks and the still-operating Pearson Airfield.

nps.gov/fova/index.htm

35

WALK IN THE FOOTSEPS
OF WASHINGTON'S MOST FAMOUS GRUNGE ROCKERS

It's no secret that Seattle is the birthplace of grunge, but you may not know you can still attend shows at the same concert venues where grunge icons got their start. Arguably the most iconic of these venues is the Moore, a historic staple of the Seattle music scene. The Moore was established in 1907 and is the oldest continuously operating theater in Seattle. It helped put grunge on the map in 1989 with the now infamous Sub Pop Lame Fest, which featured an up-and-coming Nirvana plus Mudhoney and TAB, two other bands that were part of the burgeoning "Seattle Sound" at the time. The Moore still regularly hosts well-known music names looking for a more intimate venue.

1932 Second Ave., Seattle, 206-682-1414
www.stgpresents.org/stg-venues/moore-theatre

MORE GRUNGE HOT SPOTS IN SEATTLE

Central Saloon

Located in bustling Pioneer Square, the Central Saloon is where Nirvana played their first concert in Seattle in 1986. It is also where other grunge greats like Soundgarden and Alice in Chains played early in their careers. You can still attend live concerts at Central Saloon featuring exciting local bands.

207 First Ave. S, Seattle, 206-622-0209
centralsaloon.com

El Corazón

In 1990, Pearl Jam played their first concerts (billed as Mookie Blaylock) in this venue in SoDo, though it was known as the Off Ramp Cafe back then. This dynamic music hall still hosts local acts honing their skills.

109 Eastlake Ave. E, Seattle, 206-262-0482
elcorazonseattle.com

DAZZLE YOUR SENSES
AT LIGHT SHOWS IN BELLEVUE

Visit Bellevue during the holiday season for unforgettable light shows and shopping that will cover all your recipients' wish lists. The Bellevue Botanical Garden is alluring year-round, with its wide assortment of flowers and local foliage. When December comes, though, the magic of nature gets kicked up a notch with dazzling lights. The gardens are transformed each year into Garden d'Lights, a twinkling winter wonderland with lights hung all around the property. Bellevue Botanical Garden is also just a couple miles away from another must-do light show in Washington: the Snowflake Lane parade. Every night from the day after Thanksgiving to Christmas Eve, Bellevue Way between Lincoln Square and Bellevue Square becomes alive with performers bedecked in holiday attire dancing around giant floats. The show lasts about 25 minutes, and when it's over you're right next to Bellevue Square and its many, many high-street and designer stores—all set for holiday shopping.

Bellevue Botanical Garden
12001 Main St., Bellevue, 425-452-2750
bellevuebotanical.org/garden-dlights

Snowflake Lane
Bellevue Way
bellevuecollection.com/snowflakelane

LET THE MOSAICS
GUIDE YOU AROUND TIETON

Go on a mosaic hunt in the tiny orchard town of Tieton and you'll quickly come to some of the most intriguing spots to shop, play, and dine in Yakima Valley. As the agricultural landscape changed, the town was slowly dying until a visionary entrepreneur spearheaded Mighty Tieton, an artisan business incubator that attracted a bevy of forward-thinking artists to the town, including the Tieton Mosaic Co. Tieton has since been rebuilt into a haven for artists and free thinkers while still holding true to its farming roots. You'll notice the mosaics as soon as you enter the town, since the welcome sign is adorned in colorful pieces. As you explore the town, you'll soon see mosaics pop up everywhere—on the Tieton Theatre, next to Boxx Gallery, along the side of Nomad Kitchen and Mercantile, on the signposts for local attractions, and more. Tieton Mosaic Co. also makes mosaics for businesses all around the country, including 27 for Sound Transit's Downtown Redmond Station.

mightytieton.com

TIP

A great snack to munch on while you walk around looking for mosaics in Tieton is the jalapeño roll with cream cheese from Santos Bakery.

810 Wisconsin Ave., Tieton, 509-673-0079

WATCH THE CASCADES

OF THE COUNTRY'S LARGEST URBAN WATERFALL

Spokane is known for the Spokane River slicing through the middle of the city with two dams creating the largest urban waterfall in the country. The best way to see Spokane Falls is by both foot and air from Riverfront Park, Spokane's expansive urban park that was originally created to host the 1974 World's Fair. By land, you can walk across the footbridge that crosses the upper falls via Salmon Peoples Island (Snxw Meneʔ). By air, the Numerica SkyRide is a kid-friendly option; it's a 15-minute gondola-style adventure that gives you a bird's-eye view of the river as it takes you above the waterfalls. Sit back, relax, and appreciate the special vantage point of the water. Another memorable way to see Spokane Falls is with a meal at Clinkerdagger, a steak house located in a converted flour mill from the late 1800s. The falls are usually most impressive from March through June, when rapids are higher and faster after snow runoff from the mountains.

Riverfront Spokane
507 N Howard St., Spokane, 509-625-6600
my.spokanecity.org/riverfrontspokane/attractions

Clinkerdagger
21 W Mallon Ave., Spokane, 509-328-5965
clinkerdagger.com

TIP

Riverfront Park is wonderful for families, with the Ice Age Floods Playground and splash pad, inclusive Providence Playscape area, historic Looff Carrousel, and weekend light shows at the community-centered Pavilion. "Feeding" your trash into the Garbage Goat is also sure to get squeals of joy.

FLY A KITE
AT THE WASHINGTON STATE INTERNATIONAL KITE FESTIVAL

The largest kite festival in North America happens each year in Washington. For over 40 years, kite enthusiasts from around the world have been meeting up in Long Beach to take advantage of the coastal winds and long shoreline (Long Beach gets its name because it is said to be the longest beach in the US) to show off their kite skills and fly them overhead. These are often no ordinary kites, either. You'll see colorful dragons and sea life and other giant, intricately designed kites swooping around the sky. During the festival you can watch the talented pilots compete in kite battles and the Sport Kite Stack Fly, when multiple kites are flown together by the same person. The kite festival happens each August and lasts an entire week with different events and competitions each day, plus a day you can join the fun and try flying your own kite on the sand!

Long Beach between Bolstad Ave. and Sid Snyder Dr., 360-642-4020
kitefestival.com

TIP

If the timing of the kite festival doesn't work for you, you can still visit the World Kite Museum in Long Beach, which is open year-round and has a multitude of kites on display along with information about the history of kite flying.

303 Sid Snyder Dr., Long Beach, 360-642-4020
worldkitemuseum.com

Rattlesnake Ledge

SPORTS AND RECREATION

TIDE POOL YOUR WAY DOWN THE SHORE

AT 1, 2, 3, AND 4 TOPPED WITH A JEWEL

Washington makes things easy for beachgoers with their straightforward naming concepts . . . until you realize that First Beach is not the same as Beach 1. So let's start with the number first. First Beach, Second Beach, and Third Beach are three beaches on the northwest edge of Olympic National Park that are amazing for tide pools, thanks to incredible sea stacks that become accessible during low tide. First Beach is located in La Push on the Quileute Reservation and has easy parking right by the beach. Second Beach and Third Beach require hikes to get to but are well worth the journey, since you're walking through a gorgeous, moss-adorned forest to get there. Just don't confuse these beaches with Beach 1, Beach 2, and Beach 3 on the southwest end of Olympic National Park. They are different (though still lovely). However, down there you'll also find Beach 4, which is known for epic tide pooling. Ruby Beach is also down that way and is the jewel of the Olympic National Park beach system and a must-see piece of shoreline.

First Beach: Ocean Dr., La Push
Second Beach Trailhead: Olympic Discovery Trail, La Push
Third Beach Trailhead: La Push Rd., La Push
Beach 4 Nature Trail: Hwy. 101 north of Kalaloch Lodge
Ruby Beach: Ruby Beach Rd. off Hwy. 101
nps.gov/olym/planyourvisit/exploring-the-coast.htm

MARVEL AT THE PALOUSE
WITH A JOURNEY TO THE TOP OF STEPTOE BUTTE

When the sunlight hits the Palouse just right, it seems to be awash in ribbons of gold tumbling over each other as the hills roll their way across southeast Washington. Because of the way the hills careen softly with nothing much around them, you feel like you're on top of the world while driving through the Palouse, especially when the clouds are hanging low. However, go to Steptoe Butte State Park Heritage Site and all of a sudden those rolling hills of the Palouse look far away and otherworldly as they sprawl forth in every direction from the base of the butte. Watch out for potholes as you wind your way up and around Steptoe Butte, and be aware that there are no guardrails. If you're not a fan of heights, this drive may feel a bit scary, but go slow and you'll find it's well worth it when you reach the top and see those panoramic vistas.

Off Hume Road in Whitman, 509-337-6457
parks.wa.gov/find-parks/state-parks/
steptoe-butte-state-park-heritage-site

42

GO SLEDDING
IN DOWNTOWN LEAVENWORTH

Sure, there are larger and more thrilling sledding hills in Washington, but there is nothing quite as quaint as sledding down the hill overlooking the pedestrian-only road that goes through the middle of downtown Leavenworth with its Bavarian architecture and twinkling holiday lights. Get there early the morning after snowfall so you can beat the crowds. When you're done sledding, Leavenworth is also a magical town to walk around during the holidays. Carolers, hot chocolate, and even a gingerbread café keep you in the holiday spirit. At night, thousands of lights adorn the town. Leavenworth was just a slowly depleting little mill town in the mountains until the 1960s, when locals decided to transform it into a Bavarian wonderland and put it on the tourist map. It's been a beloved Oktoberfest and Christmas destination ever since.

Front Street, Leavenworth
cityofleavenworth.com/your-city-hall/departments/public-works/city-parks/front-street-park

TIP

If you're planning to stay overnight in Leavenworth during the holiday season, be aware most accommodations in town book up early, sometimes months in advance. Family suites at the popular Enzian Lodge book up even faster—weekends usually get reserved the day they become available—which would be December 1 for the following year!

43

CHEER LOUDLY
AT A SEATTLE SOCCER GAME

What's that sound? Might be the 35,000-plus enthusiastic fans at Lumen Field, one of the most attended soccer stadiums in the US. Who are they rooting for? That would be the Sounders FC, one of the most decorated soccer teams in the country, with a loyal fan base that makes attending an open-air game at their home field a thrilling experience. But soccer is not just for the men in Seattle. The Seattle Reign are the women's team, and they also have an avid fan base and deserve every bit of acclaim that the men's team has. The Reign also play at Lumen Field and have had Olympians on their roster. Most visitors are there to watch the teams play, but Lumen Field has some perks of its own, with numerous concession stands, club seats and suites, and wide concourses that provide views of the Seattle skyline and Puget Sound.

800 Occidental Ave. S, Seattle, 206-381-7555
lumenfield.com, reignfc.com, soundersfc.com

TIP

The Seattle Kraken joined the NHL in 2021 and are also sweeping up a devout fan base. And of course, don't forget about the professional football and baseball teams of Seattle—but if you're a fan you no doubt already know all about those Seahawks (who also play at Lumen Field) and Mariners!

FLOAT DOWN
THE YAKIMA RIVER

Enjoy the blissful sounds of nature on a leisurely float down the lower canyon of the Yakima River. This can be done via inner tube, raft, kayak, or stand-up paddleboard. Whichever your mode of transportation, you'll be privy to the peaceful ambiance of the Yakima River Valley as you glide along the gentle river rapids. To enjoy the peaceful stretch of river that is without white water, put in at Umtanum Recreation Area and plan to get out a few hours later at Roza Recreation Area. You'll need a second car there waiting for you. If having transportation proves complicated, check out one of the local outdoor recreation tour companies in Yakima, such as Rill Adventures. During your float, keep an eye out on the banks of the river for elk, deer, eagles, and even cougars.

blm.gov/visit/yakima-river-canyon

Rill Adventures
509-964-2530
rilladventures.com

HIKE TO A FIRE LOOKOUT
IN MOUNT RAINIER NATIONAL PARK

Before the days of aircraft monitoring, the predominant way to spot forest fires early was to have a designated spotter in a fire lookout tower. Within Mount Rainier National Park, four historic fire lookout towers are still standing. They are no longer used to scout for fires; instead, they are now open to the public to hike to for incredible views of Mount Rainier and the surrounding scenery. Here are the lookout points, listed by trailhead name, hiking distance, and park quadrant:

- Mount Fremont: 2.7 miles, northwest
- Shriner Peak: 4.2 miles, southeast
- Tolmie Peak: 5.6 miles, northwest
- Gobbler's Knob: 11.2 miles, southeast

Hiking not your jam? Drive to Sunrise Visitor Center for fabulous panoramic views of Mount Rainier.

360-569-2211
nps.gov/mora/planyourvisit/index.htm

DID YOU KNOW?

Mount Rainier's ancestral name is Mount Tahoma and many people in Washington still call it that.

46

GO CRABBING
IN PUGET SOUND

Dungeness crab is one of the premier delicacies of Washington. During crabbing season, you'll find freshly caught crab in most restaurants, usually for a fairly steep price point. Save the money and give yourself a thrill by catching the crab yourself for just the small cost of a crabbing permit. If you're not sure where to begin, there are many informational videos online. Some of the fishing charters around the sound also include crabbing excursions. When you start looking into it, you'll find that crabbing is really not that complicated. The easiest way to crab if you have access to a boat is to head out, drop pots with the appropriate buoy marker, and bring them back. But no boat is needed to go crabbing. Washingtonians get quite creative with how they catch crab, from using stand-up paddleboards and heading out to drop pots at high tide and then back out to get them at low tide, to wading into the waves to place pots during low tide and checking them when the tide goes back out again. Where there's a will, there's a way, and once you have that first taste of fresh crab straight from the ocean to your plate, you'll no doubt become a crabber for life.

wdfw.wa.gov/fishing/shellfishing-regulations/crab

RELAX ON A SANDY CITY BEACH IN EDMONDS

Enjoy one of Puget Sound's sandy beaches without leaving the comforts of city life. One of the best places to do this is at Marina Beach Park in Edmonds, which has a picturesque beach covered in large driftwood that makes for a perfect place to sit (or for the kiddos to climb). Marina Beach Park also has a picnic area and playground. In addition to the sand, the beach looks out toward the Olympic Mountains to the west and is flanked by the Edmonds Marina, home to yachts and sailboats. You'll also see the Edmonds–Kingston ferry going in and out of the terminal. Edmonds is located about 30 minutes north of Seattle and has an artsy Main Street with lots of shops, galleries, and places to eat. Marina Beach Park is just a 15-to-20-minute walk away from Main Street.

470 Admiral Way, Edmonds, 425-771-0230
edmondswa.gov/cms/one.aspx?pageId=17292333

RIDE THE BOAT
FROM CHELAN TO STEHEKIN

Chelan is one of the best weekend getaways in Washington: wine tasting, aquatic sports on Lake Chelan, a massive water park for families, and many delicious farm-to-table restaurants. You need to add one thing to your bucket list for Chelan, though . . . and that is leaving Chelan. Let me explain. Chelan is on the southern end of the 50-mile-long and fjord-like Lake Chelan. At the north end of the lake is the tiny town of Stehekin, known for its secluded nature and refreshing lack of cars and cell service. A boat ride connects Chelan to Stehekin; the only other ways to access Stehekin are via plane or foot. Boating back and forth is long but pleasurably scenic. For adventurous souls, camp or book a cabin overnight in Stehekin and then hike back the 17 miles to Prince Creek, stopping to camp overnight along the way, before ferrying back to Chelan from Prince Creek (or do the route vice versa).

17100 S Lakeshore Rd., Chelan, 509-669-5045
stehekinferry.com

GO BENEATH THE EARTH
IN LAVA TUBES

Eons before Mount St. Helens erupted in 1980, the volcano was already making drastic changes to the landscape of Washington. Lava flowed heavily in those centuries, and the result of those molten rivulets making their way over the earth is hardened lava tubes today. These lava tubes are like long caves, and they are both eerie and enchanting to explore. Ape Cave is the standout lava tube hike in Washington. Located in Gifford Pinchot State Park, Ape Cave stretches out over two lower- and upper-level tubes. The lower level is easy to do for most age groups. The wide path is .75 miles long over mostly even terrain. The upper level, on the other hand, is more for experienced spelunkers. This part of the lava tube stretches for 1.5 miles and requires some scrambling over boulders, as well as squeezing through some tight spaces. The payoff is at the end when you reach the beautiful beam of light coming down through the opening. From there, you're back out into the sunshine (or gloom, depending on the day) and an easy hike back to the parking lot.

Forest Road 8303 near Cougar
www.fs.usda.gov/r06/glifffordpinchot/recreation/ape-cave-interpretive-site

50

WALK THROUGH A TEMPERATE RAINFOREST
IN OLYMPIC NATIONAL PARK

Did you know Washington has rainforests? If tropical "Fern Gully"–type forests pop into your mind, it's time to expand your rainforest view. In Washington, we have temperate rainforests, still known for towering, sky-high trees. But instead of being covered in palm and other hot weather foliage, these temperate rainforests operate in cooler weather and become taken over by spindly pine tree growth among the centuries-old firs, cedars, and spruces reaching toward the sky. Adding to the mystique is moss covering practically everything. When walking among the gnarled tree trunks and knotted branches, it's easy to imagine if fairies did indeed exist, this is where they'd be hiding. One of the coolest aspects of Washington's rainforests is that they've been largely untouched, thanks to the protection of Olympic National Park. Thus, you can see new growth growing over old tree stumps and trees winding together as they grow toward the light. It's truly mesmerizing.

nps.gov/olym/planyourvisit/temperate-rain-forest.htm

BEST PLACES TO SEE WASHINGTON'S RAINFORESTS

Hall of Mosses

The most famous rainforest path in Washington is the just-under-a-mile Hall of Mosses in the Hoh Rain Forest. This can get extremely busy in the summer months and most weekends. Still, it's a must-see. The forest here seems to glow, it's so green, and the trees are practically dripping in moss.

Hoh Valley Rd., Forks
nps.gov/olym/planyourvisit/visiting-the-hoh.htm

Quinault

Located close to the shores of Lake Quinault, the less-traveled half-mile Rainforest Nature Trail is also stunning with mossy, dense trees all around, plus informational signs explaining how the rainforest works and why it is important for the entire ecosystem.

South Shore Rd., Quinault
nps.gov/olym/planyourvisit/visiting-quinault.htm

51

EXPLORE THE RUGGED COASTLINE
ALONG CHUCKANUT DRIVE

Washington has miles upon miles of gorgeous coast. However, the view from the road is often marred by trees and buildings. That's not the case with Chuckanut Drive Scenic Byway. This 22-mile drive winds from the Fairhaven neighborhood of Bellingham down to Burlington (or vice versa) via State Route 11 and will have you thinking you've been temporarily transported to Big Sur, California, so grand are the vistas. Make time to stop in the pull-offs to admire the panoramic views as you look out over the salty water accentuated by the curves of the coastline and Olympic Mountains in the distance. You can also take a detour off the road down to Larrabee State Park Boat Launch, where you can park if you have the Discover Pass (a yearly parking pass for Washington State Parks and other state-managed land) and walk along the scenic beach. If you get hungry along the drive, stop at Chuckanut Manor Seafood and Grill for a meal. You'll come to it shortly before driving into the picturesque farming towns of Skagit County. Turn off for more yummy food down Edison's quaint main street.

SR 11 from Fairhaven to Burlington

TIP

On clear days, you might even be able to see 10,781-foot-tall Mount Baker from the valley during your Chuckanut drive. To get closer, another great drive to do is the Mount Baker Scenic Byway (SR 542) between Bellingham and Mile Post 58 by Artist Point Trailhead.

52

PLAY PICKLEBALL
WHERE IT BEGAN

The sport of pickleball has taken the world by storm in recent years. As it happens, an island in Washington is considered the birthplace of pickleball. That would be Bainbridge Island, located an easy 30-minute ferry ride from downtown Seattle. Pickleball got its start on Bainbridge Island in 1965 when a few friends came up with the game in an effort to keep their bored kids entertained. Pickleball courts are located all over the island, but the most memorable spot is the Battle Point Park Founders Courts, created as a tribute to the game and its founders in 2020. If you've never played pickleball before and aren't sure where to start, check out Frog Rock Pickleball. This unique tour company is run by two certified pickleball coaches, who arrange tours on Bainbridge Island that include a pickleball lesson and lots of info about pickleball and Bainbridge.

Founders Courts
11299 Arrow Point Dr., Bainbridge Island

Frog Rock Pickleball
frogrockpickleball.com

View at Cape Flattery

Snoqualmie Falls

Central Washington Agricultural Museum

Columbia River Vantage Bridge

The Palouse from Steptoe Butte

Ferry Ride across Puget Sound

Stadium High School

Boehm's Candies

Mosaic in Tieton

Diablo Lake

SHERI'S
Sweet Shoppe
Homemade
ICE CREAM
Handmade
Tamales
ESPRESSO
SWEET
Bakery
Winthrop

Mary Lou's Milk Bottle

Artists at Dahmen Barn

Novel Coffee in Richland

UPCYCLED
BOHO
BOOTS
MADE
HERE
FauxyFurr Vintage

Skagit Valley Tulips

GO SNOWSHOEING
BY SNOQUALMIE PASS

The snowy lowlands of the Cascade Range provide ideal conditions for snowshoeing in the winter months (as long as there is snow of course!), thanks to flat terrain with peaceful nature views. One of the best spots for snowshoeing is right before Snoqualmie Pass at Hyak Sno-Park. Easy parking (with restrooms) is located right by the trailhead. Cross-country skiing also is popular here, so be sure to stay clear of the groomed trail and snowshoe beside it. If you're not cross-country skiing, the trail has an option to veer off toward the picturesque lake a short distance from the parking lot. If you like to mix some food and wine into your snowshoeing adventure, keep driving over the Snoqualmie Pass to Suncadia, a fabulous resort and master-planned community that has hiking trails that turn into excellent snowshoeing trails in the winter. Snowshoe from the main lodge to the winery for a tasting or meal and back again.

parks.wa.gov/find-sno-parks/hyak-sno-park
suncadia.com

54

HIKE TO A SCENIC VIEWPOINT AT RATTLESNAKE LEDGE

You'll feel like you're on top of the world (or at least Washington) with a hike up to Rattlesnake Ledge. And unlike many other mountaintop views in Washington, this hike doesn't take hours upon hours to do! The four-mile Rattlesnake Ledge trail is located in North Bend and has one of the best summits in Washington. After hiking an elevation gain of 1,160 feet to reach the 2,078-foot summit, you'll come to a massive rocky platform jutting out to the edge of the mountain. Be careful. There is a steep cliff drop, but you don't have to get right up by the edge to appreciate the view, which extends to Mount Si, Mount Washington, and down to Rattlesnake Lake far below. Thanks to the well-marked trail and plenty of switchbacks, this is a moderate scenic mountain hike that most hikers can manage.

Cedar Falls Rd. SE, North Bend
wta.org/go-hiking/hikes/rattlesnake-ledge

MORE ICONIC SCENIC HIKES IN WASHINGTON

I had a hard time choosing just one; there are so many incredible hikes up to scenic views in Washington! Rattlesnake Ledge seemed the easiest to get to and accomplish for most people, so I went with that one, but here are some more hikes that offer unforgettable views:

Artist Point

Mount Baker Wilderness near Deming

Beacon Rock Trail

Beacon Rock State Park near North Bonneville

Baker River Trail

North Cascades near Concrete

Devil's Punchbowl

Olympic National Park near Port Angeles

Heliotrope Ridge

Mount Baker Wilderness near Deming

Hurricane Ridge

Olympic National Park near Port Angeles

Poo Poo Point

Tiger Mountain near Issaquah

Skyline Loop

Mount Rainier National Park near Paradise

55

TREK THROUGH THE ENCHANTMENTS

TO PRISTINE ALPINE LAKES

Do you like day-long, challenging treks? Then this one's for you. (If not, skip to the Tip on the next page!) One of the most coveted bucket list hikes in Washington is a through-hike of the Enchantments region. This hike is not for beginners! It is hard to do for a number of reasons. First, it takes an average of 18 hours to hike through with over 4,500 feet in elevation gain. Second, it has some rough terrain to navigate, including some scrambling, plus there's the nerve-racking Aasgard Pass, which requires skill and proper knowledge of reading weather conditions to safely hike over. And last but unfortunately not least, you can only hike through the Enchantments with an overnight camping break if you get a permit in the yearly lottery. If you don't, it's an extremely long day hike—though many people do it each year. Hiking through the Enchantments requires careful planning, research, and training, but the payoff for doing the entire 19 miles from Stuart Lake/Colchuck Lake Trailhead to Snow Lake Trailhead is getting to see the remote, rugged mountain terrain and incredibly blue glacial lakes within the Core Enchantment Zone with your own eyes.

Forest Road 7601
wta.org/go-hiking/hikes/enchantment-lakes

TIP

If the whole hike sounds daunting, consider just doing an out-and-back hike to Colchuck Lake from Stuart Lake/Colchuck Lake Trailhead or to Snow Lake from the Snow Lake Trailhead. These are still challenging hikes, but they skip the most difficult passes of the Enchantments' inner core. Still sound too challenging? Then add Blue Lake to your bucket list instead. The Blue Lake Trail is a 4.4-mile roundtrip hike near Winthrop. The hike is moderately easy with a gentle incline and the payoff of sitting at the edge of a gorgeous teal-hued mountain lake.

56

DRIVE THE LENGTH
OF WHIDBEY ISLAND TO DECEPTION PASS

Whidbey Island is connected to the mainland via the Mukilteo–Clinton ferry on its southern end and the stunningly scenic Deception Pass Bridge on its northern end. Driving between the two makes for an unforgettable day trip. Whidbey Island is one of the largest islands in Puget Sound and despite being close to Seattle feels far from city life. It's like being in the country, only surrounded by the sea. The main town of Langley has some restaurants and shops, but the real allure of Whidbey lies in the nature beyond the seaport towns. Take detours to some of the island's best beaches, like Ebey's Landing and Double Bluff Beach. Try to manage your drive so you have time for an evening picnic in Deception Pass State Park and to watch the sunset from Macs Cove next to the water and renowned green bridge.

whidbeycamanoislands.com

BIKE THE
SACAGAWEA HERITAGE TRAIL

Hop onto two wheels and bike along the Sacagawea Heritage Trail, a 23-mile multiuse trail that stretches alongside the Columbia River and connects all three of the Tri-Cities: Kennewick, Pasco, and Richland. The paved trail does a loop that takes you to some of the best sites in the Tri-Cities. As you pedal through Pasco, you'll come to Sacajawea Historical State Park, where the Lewis and Clark Expedition camped for two nights in 1805. In Richland, enjoy the scenic views as you ride past Columbia Point Marina Park, Chiawana Park, and Wade Park. In Kennewick, stop to take a photo with the 62-foot-tall Clover Island Lighthouse and then marvel at the boats stored in what appear to be floating houses in the Clover Island Yacht Club marina. Kennewick is also a good place to stop for a picnic lunch if you have kids, since the Sacagawea Heritage Trail goes right by Columbia Park, which has a popular beach and playground. Along the entire trail are spots with informative displays about the history of the area.

Parking options by the Sacagawea Heritage Trail:

Sacajawea Historical State Park
503 Sacajawea Park Rd., Pasco

Columbia Point Marina Park
Riverfront Trail, Richland

Columbia Park
Highway 240 and Columbia River, Kennewick

wta.org/go-hiking/hikes/sacagawea-heritage-trail

GET MISTED
BY THE RAGING SNOQUALMIE FALLS

Snoqualmie Falls is a massive waterfall with a 270-foot drop. This waterfall is as productive as it is beautiful, since its energy is harnessed into power by an underground generator. If you do the hike down to the base of the falls you can see some of this power plant. Snoqualmie Falls varies in its size and strength depending on the time of year and amount of recent rainfall. Toward the end of winter, after all that Seattle rain, the waterfall is massive. I've been before when the mist being made from the bottom of the waterfall is so thick and wet you feel like you're in a rainstorm and can barely even see the waterfall! There's also a cute little gift shop and visitor center to warm up in and get a cup of coffee or Snoqualmie Falls memorabilia or artwork made by the Snoqualmie Tribe, which owns the land around the falls and considers Snoqualmie Falls sacred.

6501 Railroad Ave. SE, Snoqualmie, 435-326-2563
snoqualmiefalls.com

TIP

For a heartier meal, reserve a table for the delectable brunch next door at the luxurious Salish Lodge and Spa, which looks right over the top of the waterfall.

6501 Railroad Ave., Snoqualmie, 425-888-2556
salishlodge.com

MORE WATERFALLS TO SEE IN WASHINGTON

Cherry Creek Falls, Duvall

Iron Creek Falls, Randle

Lost Lake Waterfalls, Bellingham

Lower Lewis Falls, Cougar

Marymere Falls, Olympic National Park

Nooksack Falls, Deming

Palouse Falls, LaCrosse

Panther Creek Falls, Carson

Rocky Brook Falls, Brinnon

Silver Falls Loop, Mount Rainier National Park

Spirit Falls, Cook

Walupt Creek Falls, Packwood

SKI THE PEAKS
OF THE CASCADE MOUNTAINS

Outdoor enthusiasts know the allure of hiking the peaks, but for snowbirds it's wintertime that gets their excitement flowing. There are five main ski areas in Washington, all located along the Cascade Range; from south to north: Crystal, Mission Ridge, Summit, Stevens Pass, and Mt. Baker. Crystal Mountain is the largest ski area in Washington with views of Mount Rainier. Summit at Snoqualmie has something for everyone thanks to four defined areas, though the snow can be hit or miss. Stevens is also an easy day trip from Seattle and has the benefit of fewer crowds (usually) and a great offering of runs of varying difficulty. Farther north is Mount Baker, a little over an hour east of Bellingham, known for its typical heavy snowfall. Mission Ridge is located on the east side of the Cascades, near Leavenworth, which affords it more sunny days for those needing a vitamin D fix.

Crystal Mountain
33914 Crystal Mountain Blvd.,
Enumclaw, 833-279-7895
crystalmountainresort.com

Mission Ridge
7500 Mission Ridge Rd.,
Wenatchee, 509-663-6543
missionridge.com

Mt. Baker Ski Area
Mile Marker 52 Mt. Baker Hwy.,
Deming, 360-734-6771
mtbaker.us

Stevens Pass
93001 NE Stevens Pass Hwy., US
2, Skykomish, 206-812-4510
stevenspass.com

The Summit at Snoqualmie
1001 WA-906, Snoqualmie Pass, 425-434-7669
summitatsnoqualmie.com

TIP

Not a skier? You can still explore the top of the mountains in Washington with a journey on the Mt. Rainier Gondola. Dine at Summit House when you reach the top; it's the highest-elevation restaurant in Washington.

33914 Crystal Mountain Blvd., Enumclaw
360-663-3050
crystalmountainresort.com/things-to-do/activities/mt-rainier-gondola

DRIVE THE
NORTH CASCADES SCENIC HIGHWAY

One of the must-do drives in Washington is the North Cascades Scenic Highway, part of State Route 20. Driving this stretch of highway takes you through astoundingly beautiful North Cascades National Park. This lesser-known Washington national park has jewel-toned glacial lakes and towering jagged mountain ranges. While driving through the park, don't miss out on seeing the bright turquoise hue of Diablo Lake; visit it at its base as well as from the mesmerizing Diablo Lake Lookout Point. Driving the Washington Pass, the highest point of the North Cascades Scenic Highway, is also an amazing experience. You'll likely want to pull off to take lots of pictures. After you cross that point, you'll start heading back down the mountain range and soon you'll come to the soothingly pretty Methow Valley.

State Route 20 from Sedro-Wooley to Winthrop
wsdot.com/travel/real-time/mountainpasses/north-cascade-hwy
nps.gov/noca/index.htm

TIP

A memorable hike off this road is the one to Ross Lake, where you'll also find the coveted (and hard to reserve) Ross Lake Resort floating cabins.

rosslakeresort.com

MARVEL AT THE SHEER SIZE OF THE COLUMBIA RIVER GORGE

The Columbia River Gorge makes up much of the southern border of Washington. Formed eons ago by receding glaciers, the gorge is a massive canyon through which the Columbia River flows to the Pacific Ocean. The canyon stretches for 80 miles and is up to 4,000 feet deep. One of the best places to experience the sheer size and power of this geographical area is at Beacon Rock State Park. Located near the town of Stevenson, this beloved park provides an incredible overlook point of the gorge via a narrow, guard rail–lined path winding up and around 848-foot tall Beacon Rock via 52 switchbacks. It's definitely a workout to get to the top but a doable one for most people. When you reach the top, you'll be rewarded with one of the best scenic vantage points of the canyon below. Making this hike even cooler is that when you reach the summit you'll be standing atop the core of an ancient basalt volcano.

34841 WA-14, Skamania County, 509-427-8265
parks.wa.gov/find-parks/state-parks/beacon-rock-state-park

TIP

Another incredible hike to do in Beacon Rock State Park that will take you past two waterfalls, old-growth Douglas fir trees, and wildflowers to more epic gorge views is the Hamilton Mountain Trail.

RECREATE IN THE FOUR CORNERS OF WASHINGTON

It can be quite a drive getting to the geographical corners of Washington, but each of the far corners of the state offers something special.

Southwest: Watch the waves crash against the cliffs at Cape Disappointment Bay from the Lewis and Clark Interpretation Center in Cape Disappointment State Park. Walk and bike along the coast in Long Beach via the Discovery Trail, which starts in the Port of Ilwaco, goes through the state park, and then heads north to where it ends at Lewis and Clark Carved Tree in Long Beach.

Northwest: Hike to all four lookout decks at Cape Flattery, a remote park that is well worth the winding road to get there. Cape Flattery has five wooden viewing platforms. From there, you'll see jagged sea stacks and gnarled trees covered in moss flanking the wild sea below. Get your Cape Flattery pass at the Makah Cultural & Research Center Museum, which is also well worth a visit to learn more about the land and Makah Tribe history of the area.

Northeast: The northeast corner of Washington is a wilderness wonderland that is almost always devoid of crowds. Find peace and solitude exploring the trails of Colville National Forest and get some relaxation along the Pend Oreille River, with detours to see Sweet Creek waterfall and Peewee

Falls. For a good meal after all that exploring, head to the Farmhouse Cafe in the tiny town of Metaline Falls.

Southeast: This corner of Washington is a vibrant riverbed of rolling plains around Clarkston nestled against the Idaho border. To truly appreciate the Snake River view, cross the border into Idaho and drive up to Lewiston Hill Overlook, where the river you were just driving along looks much larger and more scenic. Clarkston/Lewiston is also the area where you can link up with a jet boat tour that takes you over the borders into Idaho and Oregon, where you'll float between the awe-inspiring rock walls of Hells Canyon, the deepest canyon in North America.

63

EXPLORE THE STATE PARKS ALONG HOOD CANAL

Hood Canal is a natural water feature that, despite its name, is the only saltwater fjord in the US. Hood Canal slices through western Washington and provides the southern geographical boundary of the Olympic Peninsula and the northern edge of the Kitsap Peninsula. Hood Canal is connected to the Salish Sea, and because of its long, narrow structure, the saltwater that makes up the fjord reaches deep within the land. This creates epic opportunities for shellfish harvesting, fishing, kayaking, swimming, bird-watching, and—if you're lucky—seeing orcas. One of the best ways to experience the wonders of Hood Canal is by visiting the state parks located on its banks.

explorehoodcanal.com

FOUR PARKS YOU DON'T WANT TO MISS

Potlatch State Park

Covers 57 acres and is great for beachcombing and fishing. Also has a boat launch and is popular with windsurfers.

21020 US-101, Shelton, 360-877-5361
parks.wa.gov/find-parks/state-parks/potlatch-state-park

Scenic Beach State Park

120-acre park with a historic home (now an event venue), boat launch, and views of the Olympic Mountains. Good for picnicking and kayaking.

9596 Scenic Beach Rd. NW, Seabeck, 360-830-5079
parks.wa.gov/find-parks/state-parks/scenic-beach-state-park

Dosewallips State Park

Large 1,064-acre park with five miles of shoreline that borders both freshwater and saltwater, since it abuts where the Dosewallips River meets Hood Canal. Good for biking, hiking, shellfishing, and elk sightings.

306996 US-101, Brinnon, 360-796-4415
parks.wa.gov/find-parks/state-parks/dosewallips-state-park

Twanoh State Park

A 188-acre park next to some of the warmest water in the state and great for swimming and floating. Also has a boat launch and 2.5 miles of trails.

12190 WA-106, Union, 360-275-2222
parks.wa.gov/find-parks/state-parks/twanoh-state-park

Seattle Central Library

CULTURE AND HISTORY

64

STAND IN AWE OF AN EXPLODED MOUNTAIN
AT MOUNT ST. HELENS

In western Washington it seems like Mount Rainier is constantly playing peekaboo as you drive around. The state's other iconic volcano, Mount St. Helens, is not quite the same way. It's usually quite a journey to get a good view but well worth the effort. When Mount St. Helens erupted in 1980, it was one of the worst natural disasters in US history, causing death and destruction; the blast was so powerful it blew off a large chunk of the mountain peak and caused the largest ever recorded landslide. Johnston Ridge Observatory at the base of Mount St. Helens sheds light on the days leading up to the eruption and its aftermath, with floor-to-ceiling windows looking out to the volcano. It's incredible to see the crater up close and view the way the vegetation is still different on this part of the mountain from being flattened all those decades ago. From the visitor center, you can access several trailheads for more nature and views of the volcano.

24000 Spirit Lake Hwy., Toutle, 360-274-2140
fs.usda.gov/recarea/giffordpinchot/recarea/?recid=31562

TIP

For advanced hikers, the 10-mile trek to the rim of the crater is a once-in-a-lifetime experience.

SNAP COLORFUL PHOTOS
WHEN THE SKAGIT VALLEY TULIPS ARE IN BLOOM

Washington might be known for its towering evergreens and plains of wheat, but it also has an area that rivals the Dutch when it comes to flowers: Skagit Valley. Located about an hour north of Seattle, the Skagit Valley has a temperate climate where tulips flourish in the spring. The copious amounts of rain in the winter break to drizzles and sunshine in the spring, fostering rows and rows of brightly colored tulips. The best way to experience this is to attend the Skagit Valley Tulip Festival, when farms open their fields to guests to walk around the tulips for glorious photo ops and the thrill of being in such a colorful natural setting. One of the best spots for this is Roozengarde, the largest tulip farm in the US. During the festival, you can walk around some of those fields, then get a bite to eat from the food stands or garden products from their market.

15867 Beaver Marsh Rd., Mount Vernon, 866-488-5477
tulips.com

LEARN NEW THINGS
AT THE WASHINGTON STATE HISTORY MUSEUM

To truly appreciate all the things you can do in Washington, it's important to know the state's past. At the Washington State History Museum in Tacoma, you can delve deep into the history of the land and its people that turned Washington into what it is today. Washington became a state in 1889, and the museum covers all eras of its statehood plus the time before when the Indigenous people lived off the land. Families will appreciate the many hands-on displays and especially the vastly intricate model railroad exhibit. Other permanent exhibits fluctuate between focusing on important historical moments in Washington's past and how the art, culture, and geology of the state have helped form its present-day character. Rotating exhibits are also featured every few months, so even on repeat visits, there's more to discover about Washington.

1911 Pacific Ave., Tacoma, 253-272-3500
washingtonhistory.org

MORE LOCAL HISTORY MUSEUMS IN WASHINGTON

Fort Walla Walla Museum

A detailed pioneer village, plus military exhibits and several warehouses containing artifacts from the past, including horse-drawn agricultural equipment and wagons.

755 NE Myra Rd., Walla Walla, 509-525-7703
fwwm.org

Franklin County Historical Society and Museum

Former Carnegie library filled with artifacts and info about Franklin County with QR codes to learn even more.

305 N Fourth Ave., Pasco, 509-547-3714
fchsmuseum.com

Garfield County Museum

A collection of artifacts highlighting Garfield County's past, many of which were donated by locals.

708 Columbia St., Pomeroy, 509-843-3925
historicpomeroy.com/museum

Kitsap History Museum

Exhibits about the history of Kitsap County going back to the ice age, with an indoor Main Street replication from 100 years ago.

280 Fourth St., Bremerton, 360-479-6226
kitsapmuseum.org

Whatcom Museum

Located in Old City Hall with a focus on local and natural history, artwork, and a large bird exhibit. Lightcatcher, the art museum down the road, is covered in admission.

250 Flora St., 121 Prospect St., Bellingham, 360-778-8930
whatcommuseum.org

67

IMMERSE YOURSELF IN THE TULALIP CULTURE
AT THE HIBULB CULTURAL CENTER

The Hibulb Cultural Center is one of the most in-depth and fascinating places in Washington to learn about the Tulalip Tribe's history and initiatives to preserve their culture and sacred lands. The Hibulb Cultural Center is located on the Tulalip Reservation, which itself has a fascinating history. Tulalip is made up of six different tribes who came together to form an alliance when negotiating with the US military for reservation land in Washington plus the rights to still utilize the land beyond its borders for traditional and sacred activities. At the museum, you'll learn more about this time in history and why cedar and salmon are so important to the tribe, and you'll have the opportunity to sit in a longhouse. You'll also learn more about the boarding schools that were a tragic part of history for Native American children and culture. In the canoe hall, get up close to beautifully crafted traditional watercrafts. After exiting the museum, you are also welcome to walk around the adjacent natural history preserve, which covers 50 acres.

6410 23rd Ave. NE, Tulalip, 360-716-2600
hibulbculturalcenter.org

MORE NATIVE AMERICAN CULTURE CENTERS AND MUSEUMS

Colville Tribal Museum & Gift Shop

Lots of books, artwork, and historic info on the 12 confederated tribes of the Colville Reservation.

512 Mead Way, Coulee Dam, 509-633-0751
colvilletribes.com/colville-tribal-museum

Makah Cultural & Research Center

Beautifully curated museum that details why the land of Cape Flattery and Neah Bay is so important to the Makah tribe, including artifacts from an unearthed ancient Makah village found near Ozette.

1880 Bayview Ave., Neah Bay, 360-645-2711
makahmuseum.com

Suquamish Museum

Experience the culture and learn about the history of the Suquamish tribe at this museum. Also has a lovely garden area with a traditional mat house.

6861 NE South St., Suquamish, 360-394-7105
suquamish.nsn.us/suquamish_museum

Wanapum Heritage Center

Learn the history of the Wanapum people and their deep connection to the Columbia River and land surrounding it.

29082 WA-243, Mattawa, 509-766-3461
wanapum.org

Yakama Nation Museum & Cultural Center

Focuses on the history and culture of the Yakama people through exhibits and artifacts. Located along the Lewis and Clark Trail.

100 Spiel-yi Loop, Toppenish, 509-865-2800
yakamamuseum.com

68

VISIT THE VICTORIAN CHARM OF PORT GAMBLE

The little town of Port Gamble on the Kitsap Peninsula dates to 1853, when it got its beginnings as a thriving mill town. Today, the mill is gone, but Port Gamble is still a delightful place to meander through, with its candy-colored Victorian appeal and white picket fences. The quaint downtown area begins at the old green silos and is accentuated by beautiful Victorian homes, many of which now house cafés and boutiques. At the Port Gamble General Store, browse for gifts while surrounded by seashells thanks to the impressive collection located on the second level. Just beyond the general store is a lookout point over the harbor. Holidays are also magical in Port Gamble. The town gets fully decked out for Halloween with tons of spooky decorations and ghost tours; some of the old homes and businesses are said to be haunted! At Christmastime, over 100,000 twinkling lights line the town's many white picket fences and park areas, with events like Country Christmas that has a tree lighting and fireworks.

portgamble.com

69

IMMERSE YOURSELF IN 11 LEVELS OF BOOKS
AT SEATTLE CENTRAL LIBRARY

Perhaps the coolest example of modern architecture in Seattle is the city's public library. Seattle Central Library is a mesmerizing creation of angles, metal, and light—and anyone is free to visit, though you'll need a King County library card to check out any books. The library is over 360,000 square feet and spans 11 levels. There is even a café and 275-seat auditorium. There are plenty of spaces to spread out and enjoy a good book or get some writing done. The children's section is also expansive and bright, with tables and chairs and even a weekly Baby Story Time. Take time to explore the whole library and you'll see why it's the flagship building of the Seattle Public Library system. Be sure to walk the outside perimeter a bit beyond the cantilevered entrance to fully appreciate the engineering that went into building this unique library.

1000 Fourth Ave., Seattle, 206-386-4636
spl.org/hours-and-locations/central-library

70

TAKE A WALK
THROUGH THE PAST AT THE CENTRAL WASHINGTON AGRICULTURAL MUSEUM

This is one of those hidden gems that after you see will make you wonder why it isn't talked about more. So I'm here to talk about it! The Central Washington Agricultural Museum is an outdoor collection of farming equipment. It is the largest agriculture museum in the Pacific Northwest and has a re-created old-town main street that shows what a small farm town center would have been like 100 years ago. The attention to detail is quite impressive, as you see when you peer in the doors and windows of old-timey shops and homes. Keep walking along the museum path and you'll come to what looks like an old warehouse but is open on one side to showcase exhibits about wagon travel and what farm life was like for women in the past. Continue your walk (or drive, it's open to cars) to the adjacent dirt field that has rows and rows of farm equipment of all types and more than 150 antique tractors. Each area of the museum has a QR code you can scan to listen to information about what you're viewing. As the granddaughter and niece of farmers, I found it all fascinating and wish I could have had my grandpa with me. The steward working at the museum was also friendly and helpful.

4508 Main St., Union Gap, 509-457-8735
centralwaagmuseum.org

TIP

More curious about how certain beer ingredients are farmed? Check out the American Hop Museum in Toppenish—and do a drive around town to see all the murals.

22 S B St., Toppenish, 509-865-4677
americanhopmuseum.org

71

GAZE AT ARTWORK
DURING A VISIT TO THE MARYHILL ART MUSEUM

The Maryhill Art Museum is tucked away near the small city of Goldendale on a bluff overlooking the Columbia River Gorge. Despite its location on the outskirts, this has become one of the premier art destinations in the Pacific Northwest. Originally designed to be a mansion for visionary and world traveler Samuel Hill, the mansion plans fell through, and Hill drew on his own art and photo collection as well as his connections with friends in Europe to transform the unfinished mansion into a museum. Today at Maryhill Art Museum, you'll find numerous permanent exhibits, including 80 pieces by Auguste Rodin, glass art in the Art Nouveau style, elaborate chess sets, and North American Indigenous art. A collection of artwork and photos is also dedicated to the dancer Loïe Fuller, who helped convince Hill to turn the mansion into a museum. The property sits on 5,300 acres and includes a sculpture garden, picnic tables, and more of those gorgeous river views. There is also an on-site café with an outdoor terrace overlooking the gorge.

35 Maryhill Museum Dr., Goldendale, 509-773-3733
maryhillmuseum.org

TIP

Samuel Hill is also the man behind the creation of both the Blaine Peace Arch and Goldendale's Stonehenge replica that serves as a memorial for the Klickitat County men who lost their lives in World War I.

DISCOVER ALL
THAT FORT WORDEN HISTORICAL STATE PARK HAS TO OFFER

State parks are usually a slam dunk for outdoorsy recreation, and at Fort Worden Historical State Park that trend continues with 12 miles of hiking trails. But this state park is so much more than greenery and water views. Encompassing 433 acres, Fort Worden is an old military base that still has many buildings from when it was an active base in the first half of the 20th century, including a former colonel house and artillery museum. At the park's most eastern point, you'll come to a historic lighthouse that overlooks Admiralty Inlet where it connects with Puget Sound. From the lighthouse rolls the generous beach, ideal for pleasant walks and beachcombing.

200 Battery Way E, Port Townsend, 360-344-4412
parks.wa.gov/find-parks/state-parks/fort-worden-historical-state-park

TIP

Downtown Port Townsend is also worth an amble. Historic architecture housing cute shops and yummy eats abounds. Don't miss Union Wharf, where you can see an entirely intact gray whale skeleton.

ptmsc.org/the-whale-on-the-wharf

GO "BENEATH THE STREETS" IN SEATTLE

Discover the Seattle of yore on a tour that takes you through historic Pioneer Square—and underneath it. The underground passageways beneath Pioneer Square once housed businesses as the city folk worked on rebuilding above after a fire devastated the city in 1889. You'll learn how these subterranean tunnels were for more than just commerce, as the city regraded the land. Prior to development, the tunnels were tide flats that now stay strong against future drainage from the Duwamish River. You'll never look at downtown Seattle quite the same way after a Beneath the Streets tour. While in Pioneer Square you'll also learn about the first pioneer settlers of the area and the Native people who lived off the land before then. After the tour, spend some time walking around Pioneer Square on your own and exploring its many local businesses.

102 Cherry St., Seattle, 206-624-1237
beneath-the-streets.com

DISCOVER THE HISTORY OF PLANES AT THE MUSEUM OF FLIGHT

Washington is home to the headquarters of Boeing, so it should come as no big surprise that the state also has some pretty impressive aviation museums. One that you can't miss is the Museum of Flight, located on the southern edge of Seattle, just north of Tukwila. The museum was originally housed in the historic "Red Barn," which served as the original Boeing headquarters. The barn was barged to the museum's location in Tukwila and restored in 1983. From there, this impressive aviation museum has expanded into a multigallery experience. From exhibits about the history of air travel to the opportunity to see actual airplanes up close in the open-air Aviation Pavilion, each area of the museum will show you a different side of aviation and teach you about the intricacies of pilot life and airplane manufacturing. The museum also has a children's play area with a kid area for pint-sized pilots to explore.

9404 E Marginal Way S, Seattle, 206-764-5700
museumofflight.org

TIP

After exploring the wonders of sky travel, go to the depths of the ocean (figuratively speaking) at the US Naval Undersea Museum in Keyport.

1 Garnett Way, Keyport, 360-396-4148
navalunderseamuseum.org

LEARN MORE ABOUT
BLACK HISTORY AT THE NORTHWEST AFRICAN AMERICAN MUSEUM

In 1985, protesters staged what ended up being the longest continual occupation of a public building in US history. Why the occupation? After the Colman School (which had a large African American population) was shut down, local activists decided to occupy the building in the hope of it becoming the first African American museum in the Pacific Northwest. After eight years, the occupation succeeded, and the Northwest African American Museum has been educating visitors ever since. Depending on the exhibit, the museum can be inspiring, such as the hall of notable PNW African Americans, or incredibly somber, as is the case in the Emmett Till exhibit. Other exhibits discuss the journey on the Oregon Trail, escapes from the Jim Crow laws of the South, racism encountered in the PNW, and the ways African Americans have built businesses and livelihoods in Washington and Oregon over the past 200 years.

2300 S Massachusetts St., Seattle, 206-518-6000
naamnw.org

TIP

The 2.3-acre Jimi Hendrix Park right across from the entrance to the Northwest African American Museum was created in honor of the singer, who grew up nearby.

76

TOUR THE STATE CAPITOL

IN OLYMPIA

Travel to Olympia to see one of the most impressive structures in Washington: the Washington State Capitol Building. This grandiose building was completed in 1928 and features an incredible amount of beauty and history within its walls. The domed ceiling of the lobby is a focal point, but your eyes will quickly land on some of the building's other wonderful architectural and design qualities, like marble floors and walls and Tiffany chandeliers hanging from the Art Nouveau ceilings. To really get a sense of the capitol, join one of the free tours that depart multiple times a day. Check the schedule online before arriving. Seeing the capitol from afar is also neat and can be a great photo op. Do so with a brisk walk along the Heritage Park Trail that travels around Capitol Lake and onto the West Capitol Campus. It's a lovely setting with the capitol dome popping up behind the trees surrounding the park.

416 Sid Snyder Ave. SW, Olympia, 360-902-8880
capitol.wa.gov

VISIT THE "OLD WEST"

PIONEER TOWN OF WINTHROP

In the mid-1900s, the small town of Winthrop in the Methow Valley was in decline. When they heard the news that a North Cascades Highway was to be built that would connect the town with the cities to the west of the Cascades divide, townspeople knew they needed an idea to lure tourists to stop. The incredible result was to completely redesign the downtown area to reflect an old western town from the heyday of the Wild West. Many locals chipped in to pay for it and do the construction work. Today, there are still strict building codes to keep the western atmosphere, which is a plus for visitors because Winthrop is a delightfully fun town to explore. Do some shopping as you walk along Riverside Avenue, the main street in town. Marvel at the saloon building that survived a devastating town fire in 1893 and is now the town hall. Then head up the hillside steps away from the main street to check out the Shafer Museum and learn more about Methow Valley history.

Riverside Ave. and cross streets, Winthrop, 509-996-2125
winthropwashington.com

TIP

Take an ice cream cone break at Sheri's Sweet Shoppe, where you can enjoy the treat cowboy-style on one of the outdoor shop's saddles that serve as barstools.

78

EXPERIENCE THE GORGEOUS BLOOM

OF THE CHERRY BLOSSOM TREES AT UW

Western Washington has a climate that bodes well for cherry blossom trees, and each spring clusters of pink and white blossoms bloom all around. Arguably the most iconic place to see them in the state is at the University of Washington's campus. UW's Quad courtyard is lined by 29 Yoshino cherry trees, most of which are over 80 years old. When they're in bloom and framed by the stately buildings of the university, it feels like a fantastical flower world. Walking underneath the trees when they're in peak bloom is unforgettable and makes for a gorgeous photo backdrop. The courtyard is open to the public, though you'll need to find parking in one of the nearby paid lots or consider taking public transportation. Expect a lot of crowds on the weekend, especially on a sunny day. To beat the crowds, get there at dawn or go during the workweek and/or rain.

1400 NE Campus Pkwy., Seattle, 206-543-9198
washington.edu/cherryblossoms

TIP

Peak bloom typically happens the middle to end of March, but keep a watch on the news and social media for updates to time your visit accordingly.

79

LEARN ABOUT A SAD TIME IN WASHINGTON'S PAST
AT THE BAINBRIDGE ISLAND JAPANESE AMERICAN EXCLUSION MEMORIAL

To move forward, we often need to look backward. In the case of Washington's Japanese internment camps during World War II, it's important to remember so history never repeats itself. The Bainbridge Island Japanese American Exclusion Memorial aims to do that. Located in Pritchard Park, the monument's focal aspect is the Memorial Wall, which stretches from the park down to the historic Eagledale Ferry Dock, an important historic site, since it's where the first Japanese Americans were loaded onto a boat to be transported to internment camps after being taken from their homes at gunpoint. Most of these people were US citizens, some even third-generation Americans, but it didn't matter how long families had made Bainbridge Island and Washington their home; if they had Japanese heritage they were forcibly taken to internment camps, and they didn't know when or if they would be able to return home. The wooden panels of the Memorial Wall have the names of victims as well as pictures and artwork. Informational placards are also placed around the site. A visitor center is also in the works to be opened in the coming years.

4192 Eagle Harbor Dr. NE, Bainbridge Island, 360-386-2114
bijaema.org

WALK AROUND HISTORIC FAIRHAVEN

Historic buildings, cobblestoned streets, ivy, and flowers galore accentuate Fairhaven, Bellingham's historic village. Fairhaven is a delight to walk around, with boutiques, galleries, breweries, and cafés. Victorian-style homes line the neighborhoods around the village with peekaboo water views from nearly every street. Fairhaven was originally settled in 1853, and today it blends modern businesses with artistic flair while keeping its historic charm front and center. Check out Drizzle Tasting Room for an array of tastes via handcrafted oils above the expansive Village Books and Paper Dreams store—and enjoy a cozy meal in the basement at Colophon Cafe. Skylark's Cafe and the Black Cat are two other excellent spots to grab some grub in historic buildings. Gallery West is a great place to shop for unique artisan-made gifts or home decor. For a fun photo op, don't miss the 90-year-old double-decker bus at the corner of 11th and Harris.

fairhaven.com

MORE HISTORIC VILLAGES TO VISIT IN WASHINGTON

Anacortes

Sweet and bustling historic downtown area that often plays host to visitors before they depart for the San Juans.

Centralia

Former pioneer town with a downtown known for history-filled murals located on the National Register of Historic Places.

Ilwaco

Muraled buildings with a strong community feel and a nearby lighthouse.

La Conner

Colorful buildings right by the waterfront boardwalk.

Pomeroy

Quaint downtown area; highlights include the elegant Garfield County Auditor's Office building and Pioneer Plaza.

Sedro-Wooley

Rustic buildings and wooden animal carvings located along the streets.

Snohomish

Charming downtown area perfect for strolling and shopping, with plenty of places to eat and drink.

Steilacoom

The first incorporated community in Washington Territory, with a bustling downtown area close to the water.

ENGROSS YOURSELF
IN THE CULTURAL WONDERS OF SEATTLE CENTER

Seattle Center is where you'll find the entrance to the famous Space Needle plus a plethora of museums, theaters, and family-friendly fun. An on-site food hall also makes eating easy while visiting.

Here are some of the most notable Seattle Center attractions you don't want to miss:

- Chihuly Museum: Magnificently designed museum highlighting the works of legendary glass artist Dale Chihuly.
- Space Needle: It's worth the hefty fee to go up to the top of this World's Fair building. An extensive $100 million renovation in 2018 made it better than ever for panoramic views, with glass windows all around (and even below!) you.
- MoPop: Learn about Seattle's love affair with grunge plus many other pop culture phenomena.
- Seattle Children's Museum: Play and learning combine at this large museum tailored for children ages 6 months to 8 years old.
- Pacific Science Center: Discover the wonders of science through hands-on exhibits, a planetarium, IMAX theaters, and a butterfly garden.

305 Harrison St., Seattle, 206-684-7200
seattlecenter.com

TIP

Kids will also love the futuristic-looking Artists at Play playground or the International Fountain, which is great on hot days.

For more Chihuly artwork, check out works on display at Union Station and the Chihuly Bridge of Glass in Tacoma.

Thorp Fruit & Antique Mall

SHOPPING AND FASHION

WALK THE LENGTH
OF WASHINGTON'S LARGEST TOTEM POLE WHILE SHOPPING IN KALAMA

Kalama's Mountain Timber Market is special for multiple reasons. First, it looks out over the Columbia River. Second, it serves as a long indoor market hall with various retailers and eateries lining each side and community tables in the middle. Lastly, what makes it particularly noteworthy is the totem pole stretching above the hall. It is the 140-foot Lelooska, Washington's largest totem pole, which for many years stood tall by the riverbank. Eventually, the outdoor elements wore down the totem pole, putting it at risk for falling. The totem pole was restored by the family of master carver Chief Lelooska, though it still wasn't strong enough to withstand weather. With that in mind, a new solution for showcasing the totem pole was created: display it lengthwise and create a community-minded shopping center around it. The result is Mountain Timber Market, which has an upstairs terrace that encircles the totem pole for up-close views.

254 N Hendrickson Dr., Kalama, 360-761-3733
mountaintimber.org

TIP

Make it an overnight stay next door at McMenamins Kalama Harbor Lodge and try to find their secret rooms!

mcmenamins.com/kalama-harbor-lodge

83

FIND SOME PACIFIC NORTHWEST STYLE
AT KAVU

Innovative, durable, and colorful. The words used to describe Kavu's products could just as easily be describing Seattle, the city that has been the headquarters of Kavu since it was founded by a lifelong Seattleite in the 1990s. Kavu is famous for its rope bags, wallets, and other apparel found all around Washington in gift shops and even in REI. In addition to the bags, I love the designs ranging from mountains to orcas to skiers that adorn the company's collection of wool-blend sweaters, socks, and beanies. Kavu is heavily focused on sustainability and responsible manufacturing with initiatives to reduce, reuse, and recycle whenever possible. To discover everything the company offers, straight from the source, head to the Kavu flagship store in Ballard, or—for budget-savvy shoppers—the Kavu Outlet Store in White Center.

Flagship
5419 Ballard Ave. NW, Seattle, 206-783-0060

Outlet Store
9064 Delridge Way SW, Ste. B, Seattle, 206-456-9329

kavu.com

SUPPORT A LOCAL PAPER GOODS STORE
AT JERROL'S

Jerrol's is a bright and welcoming paper goods, gifts, and book shop that has an assortment of products you can tell have been thoughtfully chosen. Each aisle has unique items, whether vintage-style pens or wooden children's toys. The book selection is small yet manages to be inclusive and wide ranging at the same time. Friendly staff are quick to say hi and lend a helping hand. One of the neatest parts of this store is the history corner, which talks about the original owners and how the store has grown since being started in 1947. Making the Jerrol's shopping experience even better is the connected ice cream and coffee shop right by the history corner, a second location of the beloved Ellensburg institution Winegar's Coffee & Creamery. They serve up ice cream that feels like you're chewing a milkshake because it's so creamy and thick.

111 E University Way, Ellensburg, 509-925-9851
store.jerrols.com

85

FIND ARTISTIC TREASURES
IN ARTISANS AT THE DAHMEN BARN

Tucked away amid the picturesque fields of southeast Washington is an artistic haven in a charming converted old barn. Artisans at the Dahmen Barn is run by a nonprofit organization and aims to be a cultural hub for artisans and community members to come together and learn from each other. There's also a healthy dose of local arts and crafts for shoppers to browse through. While shopping you may even catch a glimpse of a resident artist working in one of the many small art studios within the barn. Walk around the grounds and property, where you'll get inspired by the gallery hall indoors and the iron fence outdoors that incorporates more than 1,000 wheels put together by the previous owners of Dahmen Barn, who donated the property to the community. Interested in making your own art? Plan your visit (and preregister) to coincide with one of the classes offered at Dahmen Barn. These classes are taught by local experts and range from pottery to cooking and more.

419 N Pkwy., Uniontown, 509-229-3414
artisanbarn.org

SHOP LOCAL
IN DOWNTOWN ROSLYN

Roslyn is a historic rail town, and you can learn its history at the Roslyn Museum. However, most visitors beeline it to First Street and its side streets, where shopping abounds. Get a latte and browse through the thoughtfully curated book selection at Basecamp Books and Bites, then hop next door to check out the fairtrade homewares and fashion from Roslyn Style and Gifts. Right next door is a cozy hut housing Roslyn Soap Company, whose owner handcrafts natural bath and body products. Across First Street is the Old Company Store building with more shops (plus a historic map and town info in the hallway), a couple highlights of which include Feather + Larch Mountain Goods, a Pacific Northwest–inspired gift shop; Fused, where a local glassmaker sells creative glass nature art; and Heritage Distilling Company, where you can purchase bottles or do a tasting. Wander Roslyn's little downtown area to discover even more shops.

First St. and cross streets, Roslyn
509-649-3105
ci.roslyn.wa.us

201 W Pennsylvania Ave., Roslyn
509-649-2763

TIP

Hungry from shopping? Eat at the Roslyn Café of *Northern Exposure* fame, or get popcorn to-go from historic Roslyn Theatre.

theroslyncafe.com
roslyntheatre.com

87

ENTER THE WORLD OF KID FUN
AT INLAND OCTOPUS

With two young kids, I've been to my share of toy stores—plus gift shops, department store toy aisles, convenience stores . . . the list goes on. For the most part, they all seem pretty similar, with comparable offerings. Which is why when I walked into the delightful Inland Octopus located within Walla Walla's charming downtown village, it caught my attention. The store was brimming over with toys and stuffies. I even noticed some toy lines I haven't seen before, and I was impressed by the large selection of popular toy brands. The best part of the store was the model train running through tunnels and elaborate miniature displays. It added a hint of nostalgia, which combined with the friendly service will have me gladly coming back to shop for my kiddos here instead of online.

7 E Main St., Walla Walla, 509-526-0115
instagram.com/inlandoctopus

TIP

If you're looking for a great toy store on the western side of the state, visit Snapdoodle Toys (snapdoodletoys.com). It is locally owned, with seven locations around King and Snohomish Counties, and has friendly service with a great selection.

DISCOVER NATIVE AMERICAN ART
AT NORTHWEST NATIVE EXPRESSIONS

Walk among the art of Native Americans and maybe even bring a piece of it back home with you at Northwest Native Expressions near Sequim. It is operated by the Jamestown S'Klallam Tribe but includes arts and crafts from tribes all around Washington. Totem poles stand proudly around the grounds, which have views of Sequim Bay, while inside you'll discover various art displays. Lithographs, paintings, pottery, jewelry, and so much more are available to browse. Some pieces also have companion information explaining more about the history of the tribes and native art in the PNW. While visiting Northwest Native Expressions, you're also close to many other buildings of cultural importance. While there, learn more about the history of the tribe with a visit to the Jamestown S'Klallam Tribal Library or a walk around the expansive outdoor campus, past placards, a Veterans Memorial, and the House of Myths, where wood-carvers work on their next totem pole or other woodworking creations. Families will also appreciate the playground and picnic tables on-site.

1033 Old Blyn Hwy., Sequim, 360-681-4640
northwestnativeexpressions.com

WRAP YOURSELF IN A WOOL BLANKET FROM EIGHTH GENERATION

Get away from synthetic fibers and back to natural materials by taking a blanket home from Eighth Generation. Started by a Native artist, Eighth Generation became the first mass-produced line of 100 percent wool blankets completely owned, designed, and sold by Native Americans. The company was purchased by the Snoqualmie Tribe in 2019 and continues to grow with a focus on natural materials and authentic Native designs. Their Gold Label Collection wool blankets are made right in Seattle, and all blankets and other products are designed by Inspired Natives®—which is their tagline to emphasize the importance of supporting Indigenous artists directly, instead of other brands that are simply inspired by Native art. The best place to get acquainted with Eighth Generation is at their store by Pike Place Market, where you can learn more about the blanket-weaving process and browse an assortment of products created by Native Americans.

1406 First Ave., Seattle, 206-695-2907
eighthgeneration.com

90

FIND A BLAST FROM THE PAST
WITH SOME CASHMERE ANTIQUING

Nestled in the eastern foothills of the Cascades is the tiny town of Cashmere. One thing that's not tiny about this town? The antique stores. Cashmere is home to the Antique Mall at Cashmere and Apple Annie Antique Gallery, two of the most extensive antique stores in Washington. The Antique Mall at Cashmere is more of a rambling mall with a cozy ambiance and a layout that's easy to get lost in as you discover hidden gems offered by a bevy of antique vendors. Apple Annie Antique Gallery, by contrast, is more modern and seems set up for serious collectors, with symmetrical rows split into easy-to-peer-into sections for a quick glance to see if that part of the store has what you're looking for. With more than 200 vendors, though, Apple Annie still takes time if you want to see the whole store! The two malls are less than one mile apart, making for the perfect antiquing day trip to Cashmere.

Antique Mall at Cashmere
603 Cotlets Way, Cashmere, 509-782-1519
antiquemallatcashmere.com

Apple Annie Antique Gallery
100 Apple Annie Ave., Cashmere, 509-782-4004
appleannieantiques.com

TIP

While in Cashmere, see an antique stove at the Aplets and Cotlets store and factory. During the week, you can watch the assembly line for these beloved treats, created with local apples and apricots. Then stock up on some before leaving the store. The slim boxes of Aplets and Cotlets make great gifts that are a yummy alternative to the ubiquitous box of chocolates.

117 Mission Ave., Cashmere, 509-782-4088
libertyorchards.com

CURATE YOUR LIFESTYLE
AT GILMAN VILLAGE

If you love shopping, you can't miss whiling away a couple hours at Gilman Village in Issaquah. It has a wonderful locally owned home goods store (Lucky Home) with a sister shop (Lucky You) selling gifts and affordable women's apparel. Several other clothing and gift boutiques are also in the shopping center, including Splendid Avenue, which imports Scandinavian apparel and decor, and CITRINE design shop for paper goods and art. Beyond the home goods and fashion, there's Paisley Parlor, an adorable tea shop with a café and retail area. Several other restaurants and cafés also help to make this an all-in-one shopping day out. While the stores and restaurants in Gilman Village are top-notch, it's also the ambiance that makes this such a memorable shopping destination. Gilman Village has some farmhouse-style qualities in its design, including a red barn door you'll walk by on the plant-lined walking path connecting all the stores. It feels like the perfect complement to Issaquah's farming past.

317 NW Gilman Blvd., Issaquah, 425-392-6802
gilmanvillage.com

TIP

For an actual farm store, head down the road to Grange Supply, a farm and horse supply store that also has an impressive toy horse selection—plus baby chicks in the spring (grangesupply.com).

UPCYCLE OLD BUILDINGS
WITH FINDS FROM EARTHWISE ARCHITECTURAL SALVAGE

Give your home some character by shopping at Earthwise Architectural Salvage at four different locations around Washington. This unique reclaimed-material store manages to be both historic and innovative at the same time. Started by a contractor who saw how much usable home material goes into landfills after demo days, Earthwise Architectural Salvage began as an effort to combat such waste. Their large retail warehouses are consistently filled with treasures that may even come from a historic landmark in Washington. Earthwise's website is impressively catalogued with many of these finds and even has a blog with info about where recent inventory came from. However, part of the fun is just showing up and seeing what treasures catch your eye, from tiles to mirrors to wood paneling, and so much more. Whether you're looking for an accent piece, doing a full kitchen remodel, or landscaping your backyard, a good place to start your design journey is at Earthwise Architectural Salvage.

Aberdeen
416 N Park St., Aberdeen
360-637-9324

Seattle
3447 Fourth Ave. S, Seattle
206-624-4510

Kenmore
6838 NE 175th St., Kenmore
425-481-0245

Tacoma
628 E 60th St., Tacoma
253-476-7837

ewsalvage.com

GET CLOTHING THAT WILL BATTLE THE ELEMENTS
AT FILSON

Filson's flagship store is a multilevel haven for those who want their outdoor clothing and gear high quality and perfectly rugged. On the way to all those intricately made jackets and flannels is a terrace with historic documents and advertisements for the original Filson wearers—men who went to Filson to get the gear they needed for Alaska before departing Seattle for the frontier to try their luck in the Gold Rush of the late 1800s. The right gear could mean the difference between life and death on the Alaskan frontier. Started in 1897, Filson quickly became known for durable craftsmanship that held up in rough elements. Filson is still known for that today, with a focus on natural materials. Their 100 percent wool jackets are legendary, particularly the Mackinac Cruiser jacket that was originally created for foresters working in the damp Pacific Northwest. That jacket will continue to keep you warm in the (still very damp) state of Washington today—and should last a lifetime.

Seattle Flagship Store
1741 First Ave. S, Seattle, 206-622-3147
filson.com/pages/seattle-store.html

94

TURN YOUR FORGOTTEN BOOTS

INTO A WORK OF ART AT FAUXYFURR VINTAGE + HANDMADE

Unless you're a cowgirl or cowboy, you likely have a pair of cowboy boots stuffed in the back of your closet that rarely sees the light of day. Turn those underused boots into a new fashion statement piece with a visit to FauxyFurr Vintage + Handmade in Arlington. It's women owned and a family affair with a 20-year backstory that shows how the couple running this store honed their upcycling and seamstress skills with smarts and dedication over time. Their specialty is taking your tall leather western boots and cutting them down into short and stylish boots that are a one-of-a-kind artwork you can wear on your feet. You can further customize your boots with adornments from their boot belt bar—worth a stop just to see the craftsmanship! Don't already own a pair of old boots? Upcycled boots that have been transformed by the FauxyFurr Vintage team are also for sale. Check what's in your size and see if any fit your style. Custom hats, high-quality western consignment clothes, and upcycled accessories are also sold.

105 N Olympic Ave., Arlington, 360-322-7322
fauxyfurr.com

95

WALK THROUGH A TOOTHED DOOR
TO SHOP AT SHARKY'S

Descend into the mouth of the ocean's most fearsome predator . . . and do some shopping. At Sharky's in Ocean Shores, your welcome to the store is through a doorway shaped to look like a shark head, complete with opened jaws and jagged teeth. The entrance is a big part of the fun of this local shop located a short walk from the ocean's edge. Inside you can browse through the standard beach town tourist souvenirs like keychains and T-shirts and mugs, many of which are (of course) shark themed. Meander to the kid section for marine-inspired stuffies and toys. Bulk candy is also available for the picking. Look up while sifting through all the beachy products to see model sharks and other coastal paraphernalia hung from the ceiling and walls. It's a delightful gift shop experience while you're hanging out by Washington's wild shoreline.

695 Ocean Shores Blvd. NW, Ocean Shores, 360-289-4462
sharkysos.net

96

FEEL SOME NOSTALGIA

SHOPPING AT ADVENTURES UNDERGROUND IN RICHLAND

You'll feel like you've stepped back in the era before smartphones once you walk through the doors of Adventures Underground in Richland. The retail space is massive, covering more than 10,000 square feet. Started by two book enthusiasts who realized their collection had grown so much they should start selling it, the launch of Adventures Underground realized that dream and then some. Within the walls are comics, vinyls, new and used books, board games, and an eclectic collection of toys and gifts, including popular collector imports. If you enjoy geeking out about your favorite pop culture media, this is the place for you. But because of its extensive offerings and community-minded ethos, everyone can find a reason to want to hang out here. Adventures Underground also has an adjacent coffee shop, Caterpillar Cafe, and a large room in the back that regularly hosts events.

1391 George Washington Way, Richland, 509-946-9893
advunderground.com

BROWSE LOCAL CRAFTS, ANTIQUES, AND PRODUCE AT FARMERS MARKETS AND STANDS

With so much agriculture around the state, there is no shortage of roadside farm stands and markets in Washington. The most famous of these is the one off a major downtown road in Seattle: Pike Place.

Pike Place Market is iconic for a reason. After all, where else are you going to find fish being thrown around next to farm-fresh flowers, artisan crafts, and the flagship store for some of the best cheese in North America? (That would be Beecher's, yum!) But there are lots of other hidden gem markets located around Washington. Some of my favorites combine local artisan crafts and antiques with fresh produce. More markets to check out are listed on the next page.

Pike Place Market
85 Pike St., Seattle, 206-682-7453
pikeplacemarket.org

TIP

Most cities in Washington have weekly farmers markets running from late spring to early fall. Search for a city and farmers markets to see what options pop up when you're there!

Chimacum Corner Farmstand

Friendly corner grocer with fresh fruits and veggies, a fresh peanut butter grinder, and local artisan soaps and other products.

9122 Rhody Dr., Chimacum, 360-732-0107
chimacumcorner.com

The Produce Market at Flower World

Located right across from its sister shop, Flower World USA, so you can do your grocery shopping and get new buds for your garden all in one trip.

19523 Broadway Ave., Snohomish, 360-668-0174
flowerworldusa.com/shop.aspx?itemid=
4067&pagetitle=The-Produce-Market

Schuh Farms

Farm that has eggs, flower baskets, baked goods, fresh fruit shakes, pumpkins, and garden gifts in a 100-year-old barn.

15565 WA-536, Mount Vernon, 360-424-6982
schuhfarmswa.com

Snow Goose Produce

Seasonal farm stand with fresh seafood, produce, artisan cheese, ice cream cones, and a thoughtfully curated wine selection.

15170 Fir Island Rd., Mount Vernon, 360-445-6908
snowgooseproducemarket.com

Thorp Fruit & Antique Mall

Three levels to explore, with produce and a coffee shop on the first level and antiques on the top two.

220 Gladmar Rd., Thorp, 509-964-2474
thorpfruit.com

98

FOSTER YOUR IDEAL GARDEN
WITH HELP FROM SWANSONS NURSERY

Can a plant and flower shop be beloved? Well, it can if it's Swansons Nursery. Located in the Blue Ridge neighborhood of Seattle, Swansons has been greeting customers for 100 years with its vast array of flora. So many different types of greenery and colorful flowers line its tables, both inside and out on the five-acre property. However, it's the people who work there who really make Swansons shine. Employees are helpful and incredibly knowledgeable, ready to help you find the plant that's best for you, whether it's your first attempt at gardening or you're a longtime hobby gardener looking for something new to grow. And no need to feel in a rush at Swansons. They even have a gift shop and a foliage-filled café, where you can get a bite to eat or a cup of coffee while you finish planning out your dream garden or collection of indoor plants. Classes and seminars are also regularly conducted for people to expand their sustainable gardening knowledge.

9701 15th Ave. NW, Seattle, 206-782-2543
swansonsnursery.com

FIND PERFECT, ORIGINAL GIFTS
AT PORT TOWNSEND GALLERY

If trying to find a thoughtful, unique gift for that hard-to-shop-for person in your life instantly raises your stress levels, look no further than Port Townsend Gallery along Water Street, which cuts right through the center of downtown. Bright and welcoming, this pleasant art gallery co-op houses the creative works of more than a dozen different artists, who rotate working in the store and are happy to tell you about the pieces and process of each artist, including their own! The high-quality art pieces for sale stand out from the competition, with surprisingly reasonable prices. You'll also appreciate the variety on display, with art types ranging from painting and photography to woodworking, pottery, and textile arts. There's even a sculpture garden in the back overlooking the water. Each artist has a section of the shop, and the work curated has an expressive Pacific Northwest vibe.

715 Water St., Port Townsend, 360-379-8110
porttownsend.gallery

TIP

If discovering new artists is a passion of yours, don't miss the Port Townsend Gallery Walk on the first Saturday of each month.

discoverporttownsend.com/art-galleries-port-townsend

100

BROWSE BOOKS OLD AND NEW
AT AN INDEPENDENT BOOKSHOP

Washingtonians love their books, and the best way to discover the next great American novel is with a visit to one of our state's many independent bookstores. We are lucky to have both used and new bookstores that are thriving and offer a plethora of different ambiences. My daughters and I adore the children's section (and typewriters!) at Island Books on Mercer Island. Two used bookstores in Washington I could easily spend a day in are Henderson Books in Bellingham, with rambling bookcases that are quite easy to get lost in, and the Dusty Shelf in Enumclaw, which feels homey and serves coffee *and* wine! I also love the pretty layout of Auntie's Bookstore in Spokane, which has mostly new books on the main level and used books along the charming terrace that stretches along part of the store.

Island Books
3014 78th Ave. SE, Mercer Island
206-232-6920
islandbooks.com

Henderson Books
116 Grand Ave., Bellingham
360-734-6855
facebook.com/
hendersonbooksbellingham

The Dusty Shelf Books & Espresso
1456 Cole St., Enumclaw
360-825-3210
thedustyshelfbooks.com

Auntie's Bookstore
402 W Main Ave., Spokane
509-838-0206
auntiesbooks.com

MORE MUST-VISIT BOOKSTORES

Arundel Books

322 First Ave. S, Seattle
206-624-4442
arundelbooks.com

Brick & Mortar Books

7430 164th Ave. NE, Ste. B105, Redmond
425-869-0606
brickandmortarbooks.com

Copper Bell Bookshop

4315a S Settler Dr., Ste. 110, Ridgefield
360-727-3151
facebook.com/CopperBellBookshop

Darvill's Bookstore

296 Main St., Eastsound
360-376-2135
darvillsbookstore.com

Elliott Bay Book Company

1521 10th Ave., Seattle
206-624-6600
elliottbaybook.com

Invitation Books

5125 Olympic Dr., #104, Gig Harbor
253-432-4566
invitationbookshop.com

Kingfisher Bookstore

16 Front St. NW, Coupeville
360-678-8463
kingfisherbookstore.com

Literary Leftovers

813 W Main St., #105, Battle Ground
360-342-8268
literaryleftoversbookstore.com

Port Book and News

104 E First St., Port Angeles
360-452-6367
portbooknews.com

Third Place Books

17171 Bothell Way NE, #A101, Lake Forest Park
206-366-3333
6504 20th Ave. NE, Seattle
206-525-2347
5041 Wilson Ave. S, Seattle
206-474-2200
thirdplacebooks.com

Trail's End Bookstore

241 Riverside Ave., Winthrop
509-996-2345
trailsendbookstore.com

Vintage Books

6613 E Mill Plain Blvd., Vancouver
360-694-9519
vintage-books.net

Second Beach in Olympic National Park

ACTIVITIES BY SEASON

WINTER

SPRING

SUMMER

FALL

SUGGESTED ITINERARIES

CASCADE SCENIC LOOP

THE FARMING WAY OF LIFE IN CENTRAL WASHINGTON

PUGET SOUND DISCOVERY TRIP FROM BELLINGHAM TO EDMONDS

EXPLORE VANCOUVER AND THE COLUMBIA RIVER

OLYMPIC PENINSULA GETAWAY

SEATTLE GETAWAY

MOUNT RAINIER DAY TRIP FROM TACOMA

INDEX